Counter-Dancing Digitality

Shintaro Miyazaki (b. 1980, Prof. Dr.) teaches and researches in the field of media studies (digitality, computation, critique, and social transformation) at Humboldt-Universität zu Berlin. Until 2020, he was a senior researcher at the Critical Media Lab, FHNW Academy of Art and Design in Basel, Switzerland.

Counter-Dancing Digitality: On Commoning and Computation

Shintaro Miyazaki

µ meson press

Bibliographical Information of the German National Library
The German National Library lists this publication in the Deutsche Nationalbibliografie (German National Bibliography); detailed bibliographic information is available online at http://dnb.d-nb.de.

Published in 2023 by meson press, Lüneburg
www.meson.press

Design concept: Torsten Köchlin, Silke Krieg
Cover image: *Latent Garden* by Aslı Dinç
Copy editing and proofreading: Rowan Coupland

The print edition of this book is printed by Lightning Source, Milton Keynes, United Kingdom.

ISBN (Print): 978-3-95796-048-1
ISBN (PDF): 978-3-95796-049-8
DOI: 10.14619/0481

The digital edition of this publication can be downloaded freely at: www.meson.press.

Contents

Preface

This book is an extended and improved version of *Digitalität tanzen! Über Commoning & Computing,* brought out in German by transcript verlag as an open access publication in November 2022. Therefore – when it seemed necessary to consider – I have put some effort into adequately signaling that some points are articulated within the context of German media theory and its neighboring fields. The arguments and points are retained, but they are situated within the idiosyncrasies of a discourse framed by a particular language and culture, as well as by socio-technological matters.

It was late 2019 when I formulated the first articulations of ideas for this book. They were meant for a volume edited by Achim Szepanski. Achim is the founder of the German record label *Mille Plateaux*, which became famous for its *Clicks & Cuts* compilation series in the early 2000s. Quickly, the idea emerged to write a longer essay. During the formative period for this book, there was a feeling of urgency, insurgency, and rebellion in the air (and also in early 2023, while writing this, activists and protesters in Lützerath in Germany, or in Peru are rising up). I presented some early thoughts in winter 2019–20 with very attentive audiences at Simultan Festival in Timisoara (Romania), at ETH Zurich, and at CTM Festival for Adventurous Music and Art in Berlin. The next step of the plan was to fully articulate my thoughts, which took me almost three years. In between, there came the COVID-19 pandemic, the acclimatization to new academic roles, and some early short publications on counter-dancing (see Miyazaki 2020, 2022). To think and practice dancing, raving, and anti-capitalist critique together is an idea which has been in the air for a long time, at least since the 1980s, but has recently been elaborated upon most lucidly by the elegant prose theory, informed by her own life experience, of media scholar McKenzie Wark in *Raving* (see 2023). My essay attempts to play different, probably more foolish, and less worldly-wise tunes with similar, but also different theoretical bodies, deriving from my rather conventional bourgeois life experience. It is therefore my hope that this book nevertheless offers some motives to start counter-dancing!

Counter-Dancing Digitality was only made possible through a great deal of support, help, and many conversations. I would like to thank Selena Savić, Özgün Eylül İşcen, Rahel Süß, Sally Jane Norman, Chris Salter, Sebastian Döring, Jens Schröter, Jan Distelmeyer, Armin Beverungen, Martin Donner, and Clemens Apprich for being open to my ideas. Some of these ideas were explored earlier at the Critical Media Lab in Basel (Switzerland) with Selena (mentioned earlier), Viktor Bedö, Michaela Büsse, Yann Patrick Martins, and Lena Frei who were all funded by the Swiss National Science Foundation (grant number 175913). Claudia Mareis, Jamie Allen, Susanna Hertrich, Johannes Bruder, and Jan Torpus were further companions during that great time in Switzerland before the pandemic. I would also like to thank Wolfgang Ernst, Viktoria Tkaczyk, and Christian Kassung for their warm, collegial, and institutional welcoming at Humboldt-Universität zu Berlin in hard times. Thanks to Andreas Kirchner from meson press for his great support and timely reactions. I thank Florian Sprenger for establishing the channel to him and Manuel Günther for providing the rough translation and base for my final polish, which was edited by Rowan Coupland. Finally, I thank my ever-supportive, understanding wife Mami and our three wonderful daughters. Without you there would be none of this.

Berlin, January 2023

Intro

Counter-dancing digitality is to be taken literally: dancing swing, cancan, or techno. But while the latter are established as types of dance and music, and can therefore be learned and practiced with the appropriate effort, digitality is not a dance, but a constantly changing condition, brought about primarily by non- and inhuman information and communication technologies. As German media scholar Jan Distelmeyer (b. 1969) pointed out in his *Critique of Digitality*, this condition turns out to be an "imposition" (2022, 1). Digitality demands and imposes itself, automates, isolates, divides, controls, monitors, prevents, discriminates, excludes, devalues, degrades, and annihilates on many levels. Just as it is possible to dance against the wind, we must also learn the counter-dance against these processes of disempowerment in everyday life! Counter-dancing digitality is therefore a foolish, jester-like wish to process, digest, and counter this imposition and to be able to shape and move it in a jointly self-determined way. This imposition should hopefully result in a positive impression, and in the same way this book is about the transformative potential and power of this wish. It will not only be about commoning, i.e., commOnism (see Sutterlütti and Meretz 2022, 141),[1] and computing, that is, computation, but about a critique of digitality that dismantles, but at the same time makes suggestions and repairs.

Counter-dancing digitality brings into view the cooperativity of digital technologies as a dynamic ensemble of spatiotemporal actualization, unfolding, and articulation and as an integrative, ever-recurring dance in the mesh and *agencement* of multiscale corporeal and environmental media – from microbes to outer space – thereby bringing itself to the fore as the modus operandi for an alternative path at the horizon of possibilities. To

1 This term is written throughout the text with a capital O in the middle to indicate the difference from the letter u in the word communism.

make counter-dancing digitality more tangible, four preliminary remarks are prefaced here: Firstly, dancing is to be considered as a communal and joint action and a body-bound articulation. Freely associated with this are processes of self-design, sometimes of individual, but above all of collective self-organization and movement. In order to dance in a self-determined way, it is not only physical coordination and flexibility that are required. Dancing is a mediated and mediating activity. Without memory and recollection, that means in short: without storage, transmission, and processing there is no dance. Cooperation with companions is critical to dancing, because no dance can be learned alone. Dancing is social. It often involves processes of loosening up structures and possibilities previously assumed to be immutable. Even Karl Marx (1818–83) wanted to make the old conditions dance. But the nature of the floor and the atmosphere of the space in which dancers move and situate themselves – i.e., their environment – affects the dance and its danceability. Political, historical, and sociotechnical contexts can all play a role in influencing the timing and spatialization of a dance. In a pessimistic view, contexts can even fully determine what is danced, and how and when this dance occurs. Consider situations that prohibit dancing or prevent it through the immobility of certain structures.

Secondly, digitality is to be humanized. This does not mean anthropomorphism, but a humanization that no longer starts from the so-called human, but looks at humanity from the small-scale, micrological view of the living, composed of neurophysiological signals, metabolic microorganisms, and influenced by biological evolution, ecology, regeneration, and adaptation. This also implies a sort of animalization, but one which is self-directed, not commanded or directed outwards at an "other." A kind of animalization which aims to be both hopeful and careful. In particular, the level of biotechnology and bioelectrochemistry connects the living, human body, for instance as an electrophysiological, somatic structure with techno-medial *dispositifs* of digitality. While here, too, the hegemonic forces of capital and the constraint of profit-seeking are at play and cause convulsions, resistance is possible by turning to the living. We can defy and actively counter the convulsions, jerking movements, impulses, signals, and rhythms of digitality through a resistant, obstinate, and self-driven dance. However, caution and care are required in doing so, because this collaborative dancing must not become exclusionary, aggressive, or even violent.

Therefore, thirdly, counter-dancing digitality is an effect of the desire to transform, in the manner of vulgar dialectics, the negativity of paranoia[2] into an ever-changing, considerate positivity. In this book, dancing is not devalued as a mania in a normative and elitist manner; it is not treated as a social pathology, a dance mania, a common disease of vulgar people, but rather articulated as a critical, open, adaptively self-organizing counter-dance, a resistance, a movement, a desire and contagion in the name of transforming society as a whole. The feeling that everything is interconnected has long since become a socio-techno-ecological fact that couples digitality not only with critiques of capitalism, the planetary climate crisis, or the decline of biodiversity, but also with the COVID-19 pandemic, the invasion of Ukraine by Russian troops in early 2022, the current and coming energy crises, famines, and inflationary waves.

Counter-dancing digitality is therefore fourthly a scenario, a program, an idea, a proposal, an instruction for a fugitive ever-changing movement forming "bundles (or ensembles) of social practices" or "forms of life," as political philosopher Rahel Jaeggi (b. 1967) might put it (2018, 29), which strives to survive the coming catastrophes as far as possible without violence, violation of human dignity, or injustice, and rather seeks to reunite spheres

2 Paranoia not only in the narrow sense as a mental disorder, but rather in the broader sense as a collective susceptibility to conspiracy theories which not only intertwine and construct everything as a hostile plot, but also foment fear, anger, and resentment, or even generate aggression.

of society which had previously been forcibly separated. The theoretical foundations for this come from two hitherto rather separate, disparate fields, which need to be intertwined and at the same time expanded by more recent positions (at least within the context of the German-speaking humanities). First, I will follow the value criticism formulated by German Marxist Robert Kurz (1943–2012) and his approaches to abolishing capitalism by means of decoupling, concepts which he developed in the 1990s (see 1997) and which were inspired by the popularization of computers and the emergence of the Internet. Second, I will synthesize this value-critical and Marxist-inspired theory of transformation with another German-speaking field of theory, namely German media theory, which consolidated itself (mainly also during the 1990s) from out of the circle surrounding Friedrich Kittler (1943–2011). My aim is to prolong the impact of Kurz's bold approaches – especially in their convincing refinement courtesy of the monograph *Make Capitalism History: A Practical Framework for Utopia and the Transformation of Society* (2018/2023) by Simon Sutterlütti (b. 1991) and Stefan Meretz (b. 1962) – by extending those approaches in terms of German media theory. In doing so, my aims can be briefly summarized as using Michel Foucault (1926–84) to energize Marx, and to catalyze the substrate with Kittler to render it ephemeral and fugitive.

I understand German media studies as a continuation of Foucault's discourse analysis, archaeology, genealogy, and critique, with its focus on the ways in which information is stored, transmitted, and processed. As such an approach it furthermore makes visible the blind spot that many theorists of the coming societal transformation address as social mediation or as a mode of relationship (see Adamczak 2017) and gives it a strong meaning, i.e., an agency that goes beyond the mere neutrality of means, instruments, and media. The instrumental application of digitality in the course of profit generation and ubiquitous exploitation is to be countered with its technological obstinacy.

While my first book, written more than 10 years ago and based on my PhD dissertation, primarily examined the technicity of digitality in terms of media archaeology, but left out the political and social, here I will not take the algorhythmic – that is, the rhythmicity, materiality, and productivity of algorithms – as a historical given (Miyazaki 2013). On the contrary, I will articulate and outline from the other direction how digitality could enable new rhythms, dances, and movements that are capable of undoing capitalism and the accompanying self-destruction of the hitherto liberal-bourgeois society and transforming it into something new.

First, a theory of cooperation has to be elaborated, one which unfolds by means of the conceptual pair of commoning and computing, and shows how value-critical Marxist-inspired theories of transformation could be updated and expanded upon in the context of digitality (Part I). The core aspects, perspectives, rhythms, refrains, and the repertoire of the counter-dance which has foolishly been demanded then unfold and are described in prefigurative terms (Part II).

The argumentation in the book is formed by an attitude that does not take subjectivation, or to put it more pointedly, subjugation by the encountered imposition as a given, but dances against it: critique as counter-dance. Here, Judith Butler (b. 1956), following Foucault, offers an anacrusis by mapping out critique, not merely as judgment and evaluation, but rather as an activity that challenges the regulating and governing structure of evaluation; that is to say, the relationship between critique and its own subjugating rules. This includes both historical-archaeological and forensic-genealogical contextualization of the respective given conditions being constituted, as well as the search for "the moments where [those conditions] point up their contingency and their transformability" (Butler 2002, 222). Critique begins with questioning the setting, the dispositif, the environment, the situation, the rules – as in dancing. To dance requires a loose, open, and adaptive attitude. As a practice of "de-subjugation," however, critique only gets moving when it obstinately practices a "stylization" (ibid., 220) that must be simultaneously changeable and ephemeral. Therefore, counter-dancing digitality oscillates between situational surveys of both past and current situations and proposals that are sometimes formulated as demands. Foucault, in *What is Enlightenment*, one of his last works, sharpened his understanding of critique, describing it as an experimental stance and "patient labor" that is simultaneously "the historical analysis of the limits that are imposed on us and an experiment with the possibility of going beyond them" (1984, 49–50). Taking up these threads, political theorist Rahel Süß (b. 1987) recently emphasized the importance of experimentation for democracy (2022, 1130). Practices of experimental dancing which are conducted at, beyond, and around limits therefore not only generate the drifting sounds in the background, but even from time to time modulate into the keynote for what I shall go on to elaborate.

[1]

Co-Operativity

Both dancing and living together are based on manifold means of cooperation. Bodily, energetic, affective, and micro-temporal aspects – in minutes and seconds – are critical in dancing, while ecosocial, cultural, and long-term effects are most important for good cohabitation. As for spatial aspects, dancing is more about interpersonality in houses, halls, stadiums, or streetscapes, while social cohabitation focuses on transpersonal events in urban neighborhoods, landscapes, or even geographic regions. Sutterlütti and Meretz make a distinction regarding relationships between one's self and other specific people (interpersonality) and relationships between one's self and people in general (transpersonality) (see 2022, 10). The argument here, however, is that both spheres are intertwined and that physiological, signal-based processes and mediations are also important for social cohabitation and, conversely, socio-organizational processes are also important for dancing. Moreover, I argue that media technologies can scale between these levels – with both positive and negative effects. Variants and dances of cooperation are located, on the one hand, between interpersonality and transpersonality and, on the other hand, between concrete and material spatiotemporality and symbolic virtuality, each of which is shaped and informed by media of cognition, memory, organization, computation, transmission, and so on. In this context, cooperative cohabitation is metaphorically composed of numerous socio-medial dance movements and small-scale, jointly-performed operations. Consequently, cooperation always involves labor-intensive actions: work, if you will. In Latin, *opera* is the etymological root of operation, but also work or labor. The Latin prefixes "co-" and "com-" mean jointly, with, together, or "in association."

An operation is generally a unit of work, an action, such as a medical intervention in a human body, a military operation, a mathematical and symbolic or a physical and material process. An operation can also be violent. There is often an executing entity, an operator, a machine, a system, an organism that performs the operation, consuming not only energy from the environment but usually materials as well. An operator becomes operative when their work becomes effective and produces operations. Through the coordinated, planned, but sometimes also spontaneous interplay of operations, cooperation arises. Piece by piece and step by step, this then generates work in the form of products, goods, and services which at the same time leave a trace behind them. Cooperativity, productivity, and mediality go hand in hand, are intertwined. Operations take place everywhere, on all spatiotemporal levels. *Agencements*, agglomerations, and ensembles of many operations form and structure themselves into an organizational unit, into a system. Work, operations, and their environment thereby inform each other. However, their relationship must be regulated, especially when it comes to reducing the negative effects of an operation.

Consequently, cooperativity in the digital is characterized by a peculiar interweaving of technomathematic, informatic, and symbolic operativity with socio-environmental and materially productive operativity. In addition, media-, mediation-, and process-oriented, highly technological aspects connect with communal and socio-political agencies. In this context, the operativity of the currently most successful and widespread forms of digitality is so powerful that it becomes recursively effective, like a fractal on almost all temporal and spatial levels. This is a depressing imposition, but at the same time it opens up opportunities for transformation! Genuine cooperativity as a state of becoming cooperative is a desirable characteristic of digitality which has so far only extremely seldom come to the surface directly, and which is largely determined by the underlying organization of computation. The great mass of digital infrastructures, applications, services, systems, and environments at hand, as noted earlier, are owned by and are instrumental to anti-cooperative, proprietary, extractive, asocial, and profit-oriented networks. Property encloses and excludes, and thus secures the power of the powerful.

Computation is an interweaving and intermingling of numerous operations and is based on a specific, computational cooperativity, which is manifested in circuits and networks according to the inscribed algorithms. Furthermore, computing and computation are, at least in terms of the prefix, etymologically related to commune, *communitas,* and communication. *Communis*, as we know, means common, together, or community, while *communicare* is to make or communicate communally. The Latin word *com-putare* means to add up, to estimate together, or to foresee, as the verb *putare* denotes to mean, to believe, to suppose, to consider, to calculate, or to estimate. Computation as a core activity of the digital is not only etymologically a communal, joint action and based on cooperation, but also from a technological point of view sometimes consists of the complicated interplay of operations of storage (archiving), transmission (communication), and computation (binary arithmetic), as well as other processes in digital hardware and software.

From a media archaeological point of view, it is relevant to take a look at manufacturing that uses workers as computational operators (also called human computers) in order to calculate logarithmic and trigonometric tables as computational aids. This was initiated in Paris around 1791 under the direction of the engineer and entrepreneur Gaspard de Prony (1755–1839). The core of the innovation was the division of labor according to principles laid out by Adam Smith (1723–90) in *The Wealth of Nations*. This manifested itself in a horizontal division of arithmetic labor to produce logarithmic tables into simple basic operations, namely addition, and at the same time in a vertical hierarchization through underpayment. It was one of the first factories of its kind (Daston 2022, 111). Thereafter, at least up until 1950, similar computer networks were implemented again and again in many variants. Such practices of exploitation through hierarchization have by no means been overcome. As an ugly innovation, they are continued under euphemisms like "artificial artificial intelligence" (AAI) or Amazon's "Mechanical Turk" (MTurk) in Jeff Bezos's corporate empire. Here, the operators sit in complete isolation from each other in front of the screen at home and perform operations whose machine-based algorithmization is still too expensive and too complex, so that human cognitive abilities are instead extracted for this purpose in the form of cheap labor. MTurk was launched in 2005 and is an online service that established the delegating of operations to be performed like machines, that is, quickly and efficiently, but in fact carried out by humans. The first application Amazon tested in the 2000s was finding duplicate listings of its own online market. Here, "divide-and-conquer" as a principle of algorithmic thinking has been short-circuited with its origin as a technology of governance.[1]

The two examples illustrate that digital, computational cooperativity can be performed by machine-based as well as by human operators and that the creativity and inventiveness

1 The artist collective RYBN has been working on the topic of artificial artificial intelligence in their project HUMAN COMPUTERS shown in September 2022 at the exhibition *House of Mirrors: Artificial Intelligence as Phantasm* in HMKV Hartware MedienKunstVerein in Dortmund, Germany.

to implement new approaches to this activity is mostly shaped by the constraints of capitalist machinery (see Steinhoff 2021). Even if the productivity of technologies increases, they usually do not bring about a liberation from labor, because capitalism operates according to the "free," self-organizing market logic, whose operativity is mercilessly oriented to profit and thereby destroys any solidarity among the producers through mutual competition. But there is another way. This dynamic and power of new instruments, machines, and technologies, which affect social relations, must be tamed, communized, made accessible to all, and set up and programmed in such a way that they operate in favor of the powerless and empower them to transform their miserable situation into a better one. My suggestion: The whole thing should be practiced as a dance! As a chorus: "Property entails obligations. Its use shall also serve the public good." How this instruction from the Constitution of the Federal Republic of Germany (Federal Ministry of Justice 2022, article 14, paragraph 2) is meant is explained hereafter.

The energy, *puissance*, and power of new technologies were already felt in the early days of industrialization around 1820, especially in the textile industry, and provoked numerous critical reactions. The Irish social reformer and philosopher William Thompson (1775–1833), for example, advocated "mutual cooperation," and opposed the principle of competition, the malignant aspects of which he enumerated with the greatest clarity in 1824 in *An Inquiry into the Principles of the Distribution of Wealth Most Conducive to Human Happiness*. Competition between individuals would not only favor selfishness over communal benevolence, making it the guiding principle of all everyday actions, but would sometimes paralyze the idle productive powers of women, making it impossible to align their rights to those of men. Competition leads to unfavorable or even unjust exertions, pains, and suffering of individuals, because the judgment of an individual is always limited and it would be much easier to cooperate. Competition between individuals also inhibits the spread of common knowledge through the need for secrecy, when achievements in science, art, and community life are subordinated to individual gain (Thompson 1824, 369). In a society operating on the principle of competition, any improvements in production would always benefit the capitalists rather than the unsuspecting worker or the consumer (ibid., 532). Equitable and reciprocal cooperation, on the other hand, would not only prevent the waste and unnecessary expenditure of labor power for which there is no demand in the market, it would also prevent the losses of the many in the name of the profit of the few, as well as life, health, and pleasure being wasted through poverty, ignorance, and neglect. Additionally, it would distribute production and consumption equally and thereby make it possible for everyone to have a livelihood (ibid., 393).

Commons

It is not just since the 1820s that people have been dreaming up societies based on equitable cooperativity. On the contrary, with the emergence of capitalism and "modernity," they were rather almost completely eliminated in Europe at that time. Already 600 years earlier in England were such forms of cooperation called *commons*. Here, too, the etymological relationship to *communitas*, commune, and communication applies. As the plural of *common*, meaning ordinary, general, communal, the term commons applied not only to goods, animals, or landscapes, but also to people. The phrase "enclosing commons," which appears for example in the English Parliament's Commons Act of 1235, entailed the enclosing, fencing-off, capture, and appropriation by feudal lords of forests and fields that were communally maintained and used. The English Parliament was established a few decades earlier to strengthen the barons and act as a counterweight to the House of Plantagenet. Members of this French-born ruling dynasty sat on the English throne for many years. As the Marxist social historian Peter Linebaugh (b. 1942) pertinently outlined, it is important here to remember the Magna

Carta – an agreement written in 1215 and recognized by the young Henry III in 1217 – because it was not only intended to weaken the power of the king and strengthen the rights of the feudal lords and tradesmen, but it incidentally declared the forests as commons, which was additionally quoted in chapter 47 of the Carta and the accompanying Carta Foresta of 1217 (see Linebaugh 2008, 28, 42). Forests have always provided important resources for the rural population, not only for dwellings and everyday items, but above all as suppliers of energy. Viewing the forest as a commons, however, was an ancient relic of long-bygone ways of life. With comprehensive deforestation by the eighteenth century, especially on the English Isles, coal became necessary as a source of energy. What might have happened if the forests had remained commons? It's a question that so many counter-narratives could address.

It was above all the Enclosure movement of the sixteenth century which saw the forests, together with the pastures, forcibly taken into the possession of the rulers as property – as a land grab, if you will. In *The Great Transformation,* the famous social and economic historian Karl Polanyi (1886–1964) already impressively described how the pastures provided the infrastructure for sheep wool production and the basis for a "revolution of the rich against the poor" (1944, 35). Marxist economic geographer David Harvey (b. 1935), discussing Marx's *Capital*, described this change as "a systematic theft of communal property" (2018, 297) and a transition "from a world in which 'community' is defined in terms of structures of interpersonal social relation to a world where the community of money prevails" (ibid, 296). Marx himself called the wealth and capital from such violent expropriations "primitive accumulation" (1976, 874) that arises with the "historical process of divorcing the producer from the means of production" (ibid., 875). Feudal lords deprived peasants of their productive assets by privatizing the forests and fields, i.e., the commons, that they had shared, so that they could no longer support themselves and consequently were forced into waged factory work. Landless peasants thus became working machines.

Silvia Federici (b. 1942), political philosopher and feminist, offers an illuminating explanation: Capitalism can be seen as a counter-revolution against the emerging free society of the late Middle Ages. The period after the plague from 1350 to about 1525 is considered to be the peak of peasant wealth in Europe, because the decline in population due to mass deaths meant that the peasants could always maintain the wages they received from the feudal lords, since for a long time there were too few peasants, but the lords still needed food (see 2004, 45). With the population growth in the sixteenth century, this situation deteriorated again, and at the same time the feudal lords became increasingly powerful. The *Twelve Articles of the Peasantry in Swabia* of 1525, printed almost 25,000 times as a pamphlet in the midst of the German Peasants' War, demanded, among other things, the conversion of forests, meadows, and fields back into commons, but it was far too late for that. The peasants' uprisings were quelled everywhere. Alongside them, however, it was above all enlightened, knowledgeable, and wise women who were a thorn in the side of the church and the feudal lords. Reproductive knowledge, such as contraception, as a common good or commons, was soon demonized and deliberately suppressed. The witch burnings and peasant uprisings of the fifteenth to seventeenth centuries are symptoms of a long, violent, sociopolitical process of differentiation that not only transformed the bodies of formerly self-sufficient people into working machines, but also deprived women in particular of their freedoms and cultures of knowledge and condemned them to being reduced to the reproduction of working machines (see ibid., 63).

The dawn of early capitalism is an intriguing depository of forgotten contexts of Europe's past and at the same time offers eye-opening parallels to the transformation processes of recent decades. Moreover, this period is also pertinent to a critical cultural archaeology of dance. Dancing in this transitional period was often described in the context of its power and danger, as a trigger for contagious movement. This refers to dances located in a peculiar tension between mass religious movement, revolt, ecstasy, and disease. In 1374 such dances were observed in the Rhineland and in 1518 in Strasbourg. Usually called *Veitstanz* or also *Johannistanz* by contemporary witnesses, these "more or less similar cases of involuntary physical expressions, individual, or even collective dances" (Rohmann 2013, 16, my translation) were not called dancing mania until the nineteenth century. In 1832, still within living memory of one of the first cholera pandemics in Europe, appeared *Die Tanzwuth: Eine Volkskrankheit des Mittelalters* by Justus Hecker (1795–1850), probably the world's first university professor in the field of history of medicine, establishing the idea of dance mania as an effect of pathological sympathy (see ibid., 39).

Positive appreciations of dance mania before 1900 are rare, and it would certainly be more insightful to listen to the past and short-circuit its history with that of the techno rave.[2] At the latest it was with Friedrich Nietzsche (1844–1900) that a positive interpretation of dance mania first came about. In 1872, in *The Birth of Tragedy Out of the Spirit of Music*, he referred directly to the Dionysian power of the collective dances of the late Middle Ages (see ibid., 55) and criticized scholars and scientists who:

> from lack of experience or from stupidity turn away in contempt and pity from such phenomena as they would from "folk diseases" with a greater sense of their own good health. (Nietzsche 2000, 22)

2 The renowned artist and scholar Hito Steyerl referred to dance mania in an artwork lucidly reflecting contagion in terms of an info-demic, where she worked with computational models designed by Ayham Ghraowi simulating how dancing spreads in a rave of strangely drunken policemen (see Ghraowi 2020). In November 2020, I had the pleasure of taking part in the first episode of *Hito Steyerl 4 Nights at the Museum, A weird-ass visual podcast* to discuss with Hito and Ayham this work shown at the exhibition *I Will Survive* at K21 in Düsseldorf.

This brings the 500-year arc back to the nineteenth century: The disappearance of the commons, the common goods, the free forests, fields, and proto-feminist knowledge cultures, as well as many an ecstatic mass dance in the eighteenth century, set the stage for the emergence of the class of the dispossessed, the proletariat, who could only sell their labor and reproductive power. A look back at just one tenth of this extensive arc, that is, 50 rather than 500 years (the period from 1970–2020), shows that the idea of the commons, though weakened, is far from completely forgotten. As long as this is still the case there is hope.

Commoning

The vectorial power that governs digital technologies, communications infrastructures, and server farms has spawned, in the early 2020s, a planetary ulcer of computational power from only a few companies – we affectionately call them GAFAM (Google, Amazon, Facebook,[3] Apple, Microsoft). This "form of power of its own variety," according to literary scholar and archaeologist of the present Joseph Vogl (b. 1957), operates by intertwining "sovereign prerogatives, governing actions, business transactions, and market operations" and generating its own rules, axioms, and dependencies, which he calls "cosmopolitan," unbounded "energy," drawing on formulations from Marx (Vogl 2022, 11; Marx 1975, 342). The Marxist media scholar McKenzie Wark (b. 1961) provocatively proclaimed the death of capitalism some years ago – capitalism which has become so powerful in the last five to 10 years that it might have to be called something else. Recently, not only work or leisure, but also our "sociability" (2019, 3) and our sense of community, which is generated in a mediated and designed everyday life, gets measured, calculated, exploited, extracted, and captured.

3 Facebook Inc. rebranded itself as Meta Platforms in 2021.

This *puissant* development must be reversed, according to the insistence and foolish wish of this book. When parts of human sociality are computed, digested, and extracted by social media, digital networks, platforms, and other forms of opinion exchange, then it is necessary to take critical and vigorous countermeasures, to resist, to reclaim what has been lost, to think in another way, and to take other paths. New forms of genuine sociality, which at the same time do not exclude but rather include everyone who wants to be included, must be implemented. Commoning is one of the approaches that has often been cited lately, but, as has been explained, it is also one of the oldest.

Commoning refers to successful, solidarity-oriented cooperativity in operation, which is at the same time a form of sharing, communicating, but also of inclusive co-sharing or com-puting. Commoning is a semantic neighbor of commune, computation, and communication. Communication is not an immaterial process, but a materialistic-energetic one, yet intertwined with technomathematics. Operations of calculation – computation in computers and in networks – are based on both human and non-human technological processes that generate signals and data that are shared and managed within a network and that could be considered digital commons. Now that everything can be digitized, theoretically it can all be transformed into a digital commons. Because private property is abandoned in the process, the transformation into a commons, strictly implemented, prevents a digital copy from being destroyed for no reason and without the consent of all involved.[4] Personal data would not, of course, be part of the commons in principle, but only with the consent of all involved parties and under certain conditions.

The connection between commoning and computing, however, goes much deeper. For even the scholarly or academic position

4 *Abusus* in ancient Roman law entailed practices of destruction without any reason, when concerning the free citizen, family patriarch, or landowner.

of commoning is sometimes coupled with the emergence of the personal computer, new telecommunication networks, and computational practices during the 1980s and 1990s. In 1990, Elinor Ostrom's (1933–2012) *Governing the Commons* was published, a book in which the political scientist and economist not only updated the notion of the commons with her concept of "common pool resources," but also drew on game theory to technomathematically model the idea of the commons in the field of governmental science and governance. Ostrom's theory of the commons was, in fact, neither Marxist, nor sociological, nor cultural studies, nor post-structuralist. As a result, her research on the commons was received primarily by the so-called sciences of government and governance (law, economics, policymaking, statistics). Widely read and further developed, her work was awarded the Nobel Prize in Economic Sciences in 2009, in the midst of a financial crisis. Ostrom thereby simply confirmed long-forgotten knowledge, as in my opinion her most important contribution to the theory of the commons was an insight that had already become apparent with the aforementioned Magna Carta, namely that commons must always be normatively created by law or legal ruling and their accessibility must be assured. Ostrom described it all in the shadow of the episteme of "institution," a key concept in New Institutional Economics (NIE), which from the late 1970s gained prominence through the work of Oliver E. Williamson (1932–2020).

The liberal economist Douglass C. North (1920–2015) described the study of contracts as the core of this NIE. According to his theory, institutions were not persons, not even legal persons, but rules and habits that provided individuals with incentives and warning signals regarding their economic behavior (see 1986, 231). The change in these rule structures is called institutional change and also causes a transformation, both of economic activity and of the behavioral patterns of all participants. Consequently, it was the easy-to-understand and simply-formulated design principles that made Ostrom's *Governing the Commons* popular. Among them were rules and organizational principles such as the clear demarcation of what belongs to the commons and what does not, the principle of the primacy of communal decisions (including rule changes, rules for violations, and simple conflict resolution mechanisms), and mutual recognition or embedding in larger communal networks (see 1990, 90). Ostrom's focus on rules and organizational principles in particular could make her a discourse analyst following in Foucault's footsteps; at the same time, commoning and computing should have moved closer together in her theories on this. However, this happened later, and not all at once, but rather in stages. The groundwork for this long-overdue synthesis, however, had already been laid in the late 1990s.

Computation, meanwhile, played a purely analytical, rather than a synthetic and operational, role in Ostrom's research, which was probably conducted mainly in the 1980s. That is to say, it acted to model game theory, primarily to argue against the prisoner's dilemma, the famous thought experiment. This dilemma models the situation of two prisoners who are accused of committing a crime together, but who are interrogated individually and cannot communicate with each other in the process. If they both deny the crime, they both get a lighter sentence because they can only be proven to have committed one crime, which is punished less severely. If they both confess, they both receive a high penalty – but not the maximum penalty, because of their confession. If, however, only one of the two prisoners confesses, this prisoner will go unpunished as a key witness, while the other will receive the maximum penalty as a convicted offender who did not confess. The dilemma now is that both must decide either to deny their crimes, and cooperate with the other, or to confess and betray the other. All of this must be decided without knowing the other prisoner's decision. The dilemma is designed to perfidiously demonstrate how decisions which are rational on an individual basis can lead to collectively worse outcomes and thereby challenge our belief in absolute truths. The dilemma could be solved mathematically, but first Ostrom argued for a critical look at the modeled situation itself: Viewing individuals as prisoners each in isolation is unproductive and restrictive; instead, through institutional change (i.e., by changing the rules and operativity), the restrictions inherent to the prison as institution should be changed in such a way that they become more acceptable or are removed altogether, and that there is an overall increase in self-determination for all participants. This, she argues, could also prevent the "tragedy of the commons" as popularized by the pessimistic right-wing conservative and social biologist Garrett Hardin (1915–2003) in the late 1960s (Ostrom 1990, 7).

That Hardin's tragedy of the commons is mentioned together with the prisoner's dilemma and game theory seems to be an effect of later discourse production. Published in December 1968 in the prestigious journal *Science*, the article primarily addressed the problem of population growth, which in his view needed to be stopped in view of the planet's limited resources. This was, according to Hardin, not an optimization problem, but a moral issue. Hardin thus pointed to John von Neumann (1903–57) and Oskar Morgenstern (1902–77), who had proved that it was impossible to optimize two or more variables simultaneously. The reference to game theory is not in the running text, but in the bibliography, where *The Theory of Games and Economic Behavior*, published in 1944, was listed.

Hardin did not rely on economic rationality, but on natural selection and moral weighting, because only the establishment of mutually coercive relationships would be successful. Hardin's conservative morality went so far as to demand that the right to childbearing no longer be regarded as a commons (see 1968, 1248, 2nd column). Hardin's right-wing critique of bourgeois liberals and their belief in an "invisible hand," organized in a decentralized fashion, and that would steer rational actions in the right direction as an aggregation effect, is to be classified accordingly. It assumes that there is no rationality as such, because everything has to be enforced in morally-normative terms. All these highly questionable arguments are not mentioned by Ostrom, nor others who reference Hardin. In the game theory underpinnings of Hardin's "Tragedy of the Commons" from the 1970s onward, we can thus assume a techno-scientific whitewashing of a right-wing conservative ideology.

The operative and mediating component of computation found its way into the realm of the commons at the latest with the spread of the Internet from the 1990s onward. Commoning could not only be computed algorithmically in the form of models, but also performed, timed, and sometimes self-rhythmized algorithmically. Legal and computational agencies, i.e., laws, rules, institutions, and algorithms, protocols, and codes thereby continuously converged. It was probably no coincidence that Yochai Benkler (b. 1964), a legal scholar, called the "digital" variant of commoning "commons-based peer production." The fact that he had not already articulated his theory in the 1990s, but only at the end of 2002, right in the near-forgotten interim period after September 11th and the final bursting of the dotcom bubble, was due to the historical situation in which he found himself. For it was precisely in this brief period of the 2000s, a decade before the rise of GAFAM, that commons-based peer production seemed to offer a serious alternative to purely profit-oriented modes of production. In the background to Benkler's investigation are the new forms of networked exchange, knowledge dissemination, and free software, also called Free/Libre and Open Source Software (FLOSS), that became available via the Internet. The success of GNU/Linux, a computer operating system that has been freely accessible as open program code since 1992 and may thus be further developed in a decentralized manner, showed how powerful alternative modes of production can become. This was proven, for example, in the fact that around the year 2000, the use of GNU/Linux as an operating system for servers – combined with Apache, MySQL, and PHP – became the standard design for web servers worldwide. For a short time it seemed possible and self-evident that in the near future all knowledge and all information goods would become commons and would be forever liberated from ownership.

Benkler's "Coase's Penguin, or, Linux and *The Nature of the Firm*" was published in 2002 in the *Yale Law Journal*, one of the most prestigious journals in legal scholarship, and can thus be situated as an ambivalent analysis of the aforementioned phenomena both on the side of the new commons-oriented modes of production and on the side of bourgeois-liberal capital and governmental science. Despite its ambivalence, the article became a reference text for the alternative digital commons movement, because in it Benkler elaborated in detail that commons-based peer production is based on organizational principles that resemble neither those of a firm nor those of the free market, but rather take a third path. By this he meant modes of organization that are determined neither by predetermined hierarchies and top-down rules – as is common in large firms – nor by free-market control mechanisms based on prices and processes of exchange. Instead, he argued, they are characterized by joint, equal collaboration, the pursuit of common interests, and the voluntary sharing and exchange of information.

According to Benkler, collaborative production networks would, above all, re-address an old information problem: How do collaborators know what to do to be most productive? How can problems that can be solved well in interpersonal communities also be addressed at the transpersonal, societal level? The free market solves this problem in a self-organizing way: First, answers are sought in prices and market values and, second, the reduction in complexity effectuates that everyone knows what to do. Companies solve this problem by having managers select the best options from the various possibilities and by operating along the chain of command according to their instructions (see 2002, 375). Here, the manager centrally regulates what is to be done in the team. The company thus hedges the possibilities and structures them. The market structures itself through a process of simplification which lets market participants make their own decisions. Dynamic transactions and allocations of finance emerge.

What if production systems, such as the company and the free market, are literally understood as information networks (see Beverungen et al. 2019, 1, 7)? This is no longer a question of communications engineering, but rather an issue of computational, operational synthesis: an issue of modeling. A company operates with pre-structured "channels," which as infrastructures are static and relatively inflexible, but profit-optimized, whereas on the free market the "channeling" is dynamic depending on prices (it becomes more like routing) and is produced at short notice in each case by a widely ramified network. Yet the costs of establishing the connections are relatively high. In free markets, messages are property, they must be transmitted securely and in pristine condition from A to B, and the whole process often has to be contractually regulated. These high connection costs were described as early as the 1930s by British economist Ronald Coase (1910–2013) in *The Nature of the Firm*. According to Benkler, Coase argued that firms can reduce these costs (later called transaction costs). This, in terms of economic theory, established the legitimacy of large companies.

That was in the 1930s. Commons-based peer production, however, has the following advantages over the market and firms, according to Benkler: In order to solve the issue around obtaining the correct information, peer production is based (in a similar way to the free market) firstly on decentralized information storage and transmission (see ibid., 375); and secondly there would be no restrictions on commons, since they are accessible to all and community-oriented, and thus they reduce transaction costs. Within free markets this is done while enclosing information as property. Combined with the competitive situation, this builds an obstacle to a barrier-free transmission process (i.e., increasing transaction costs). In commons-based peer production, participants decide for themselves and in a decentralized manner which task is to be carried out and which is not.

Thirdly, it is important to introduce rules and mechanisms to prevent recurring wrong decisions:

> Peer production provides a framework within which individuals who have the best information available about their own fit for a task can self-identify for the task. This provides an information gain over firms and markets, but only if the system develops some mechanism to filter out mistaken judgments that agents make about themselves. (Ibid., 376)

The increase in transaction costs incurred are low compared to those incurred by ownership and enclosure. But there is also here an increased personal responsibility for each participant, therefore appropriate learning opportunities would need to be provided. Pedagogical knowledge and strategies become critical here, as is having the ability (and composure) to deal with complexity. In this sense, in peer production there are ideally no more simple decision-making principles, as they are still located within the market which is geared towards equilibrium. The fact that all this is not easy to manage is shown by the many failures in this area.

While information and knowledge have always been rather loosely coupled with resources, the costs for their production, storage, transmission and processing had been rather high until the 1980s. With the subsequent increase in digitization, the situation changed: Storage media, computers, screens, and other devices became cheaper. Transaction costs were massively reduced. According to Benkler, this is what distinguishes commons-based peer production in and through the Internet from the material commons of woods or fish described by Ostrom. Transaction costs, however, have always been reduced only superficially, for in fact they are merely made invisible through externalization, that is, through deferral and cover-up.

As previously noted, Benkler, a legal scholar, also worked to the benefit of powerful companies or government bodies by, in the aforementioned article, repeatedly recommending ways for companies to make profits in spite of FLOSS and peer production. These recommendations included indirect appropriation processes, i.e., by focusing on hardware, which has for example been Apple's profit strategy since 2007. His references to productive strengths and the increase of productive power in the field of knowledge production through projects like NASA Clickworkers is to be understood as directly "passing the ball" to profit-seeking companies. To cite NASA Clickworkers as an example of scientific knowledge production was probably not malicious. However, from today's perspective, the name of this project bears dangerous similarities to approaches that have also found their way into recent digital capitalism through Big Tech companies like Amazon, especially in the aforementioned MTurk platform.

Pablo Velasco González, a Mexican scholar of digital culture, and the Swedish-Australian media scholar Nathaniel Tkacz (b. 1981) touch on this issue in the course of their lucid analysis of blockchain technology:

> What seems pertinent is that peer production offers no clear guarantees in terms of a pathway out of market societies. … It can be made to fit very well within existing liberal economic ideals (Benkler), and actual instances of peer production can easily be deployed to produce their others, that is, peer technologies can become market technologies. (2021, 244)

How can we make sure that not-for-profit technologies do not turn back into profit-oriented ones? Because this is exactly what has happened in the meantime.

More than 20 years after the publication of "Coase's Penguin, or, Linux and *The Nature of the Firm*" in 2002, the realization of the dream for the worldwide spread of the peer production principle seems further away than ever. The uncanny rise of GAFAM since 2015 from the ruins of the 2007–10 financial crisis and the strengthening of the right, accelerated by the so-called "refugee crisis" and the triumph of a few Big Data-driven "social" networks that have accelerated a social fragmentation and polarization, shows that commoning can only spread and flourish as a practice when certain insights attain a critical mass. These insights could for example be that the current "system" cannot continue, that both technophobia and technosolutionism need to be avoided, and finally that knowledge needs to be accessible and openly protected for all.

Accordingly, we must finally start to intervene while dancing! However, before approaches, ideas, directions, and reflections on this are articulated in Part II (counter-dance), intertwined thinking will be practiced, and the modulating prefiguration of commOnism with computation – very much in the spirit of commoning & computing – will be demonstrated. For this purpose, in a further section, some of the most important threads of discourse of the last 25 years will be drawn upon, in order to still have time to conjure up the counter-dance.

Computation and CommOnism

To concretize computation as commOnistic cooperativity is to start with the realm of operations and uncover some of the more accessible layers of profit-oriented cooperativities. This firstly means operations such as dominate, destroy, extract, correlate, discriminate, exclude, or ignore. Secondly, they are based on supposedly neutral operations such as regulate, compare, scale, or dissect. Thirdly, these are in turn composed of basic arithmetic operations such as add, subtract, multiply, and divide. The differentiation of profit-oriented, competition-reinforcing cooperativity into three different layers and encapsulations emphasizes the intermediate transitions together with the infusion of the intentional instrumentality located in each. Subtraction is performed in order to compare, to be able to exclude, ignore, or discriminate later. Ability is power or simply capacity as wealth, and what can be excluded can also be extracted, isolated, and governed in order to be further exploited elsewhere as raw material. In private property, as real estate and as private wealth, it can be exhausted and destroyed without any legitimization (see Redecker 2020, 28). Therefore, it is to be expropriated everywhere that it would be useful for society as a whole.

Furthermore, multiplication is done in order to scale, in order to correlate from which rules are formed, in order to compare, and in order to ultimately extract again, i.e., to exploit or to devalue, perhaps even to destroy (on the topic of correlation, see Chun 2021, 52). It is important to emphasize here that the connection of the different operations from the three layers is contingent and thus may be made in a different way. Subtraction can also be done in order to compare, but then not to exclude or ignore, that is, neither to devalue or destroy, nor to exploit, but to secure the resource in an open and protected way and make it accessible to all as commons.

A social fabric based on commons is what I call commOnistic. It should be emphasized that the commons includes not only the technical and logistical means of production, but at the same time resources and materials in order to produce. Both material and immaterial, less energy-consuming, quasi-symbolic resources are meant here, embedded in both organic and non-organic bodies, operativities, institutions, circuits, networks, channels, and feedback control systems.

Operations like multiplying and correlating, but also those such as optimizing or accelerating can *also* operate in terms of commOnization, i.e., instead of the usual infinite profit, they can equally strive for the never-ending solidarization of all planetary processes, organisms, and matter as the ultimate goal. CommOnization as an operation means two things: first, the exclusion of exclusion, and second, eternal connectedness. If this is even more generally formulated, this would entail (digitalized) work processes, operativities, tasks, solutions, methods, rules, protocols, laws, agreements, contracts implemented in algorithmic operativities, as code and (legal) codex in execution. These must not, however, lead to knowledge, data, things, or resources as commons being enclosed, excluded, made invisible, inaccessible, no longer discussable, unchangeable, declared final, or even violently defended as property. Data and algorithms, resources and operations must not be devalued into mere isolated instruments. They are, to repeat the point, embedded in their environments and contexts. The more complicated their design and programming, the higher the potential for them to exhibit an obstinacy, a willfulness, an agency and a logic of their own that is diametrically opposed to the original intentions of the developers. Formulated in more general terms, the instrumentalization, the forcefully reduced use of computation for specifically defined purposes already seems to form a limitation of its manifold, often undiscovered potentials. Such potentials become visible during longer practice and examination of an instrument, for example a procedure of algorithmic face recognition, a communications network, the use of dating apps, or a delivery service. Instruments can be used to accomplish things that were probably not intended when they were produced. Instruments can be used differently. It is often moments of breakdown, disruption and failure, *glitches*, that bring out that obstinacy, willfulness, waywardness, that inherent logic. However, all of this can only unfold within a framework that is not only beyond profit orientation, but at the same time, through appropriate measures, agreements, contracts, rules, protocols, and algorithms, excludes the possibility of exclusion. Only under such commonly set frameworks can dysfunctional computation be tolerable and indeed valued. It is therefore no coincidence that the concept of obstinacy – as developed by German Marxist scholars such as Oskar Negt (b. 1934) and Alexander Kluge (b. 1932) in their monumental 1981 monograph *History and Obstinacy* – has been taken further into the realm of media art theory, more specifically by Swiss art theorist Giaco Schiesser (b. 1953). He conceptualized obstinacy (*Eigensinn* in

German),[5] as a power in artistic production (2005; see also Kluge and Negt 2014, 292).

Exclusion is an operation of absolute brute force. It can lead to loss and destruction. However, avoiding exclusion does not mean that everything should now be littered, clogged, and jammed. Data storage is limited. Waste is to be avoided. Enormous mountains of waste are only possible under capitalism. Resources that are no longer needed are kept in circulation sustainably in the commOnistic cooperativity according to the principle of recycling and circularity: they are either reused, repurposed, or ideally decomposed until they are no longer toxic and can no longer decay. The systems should no longer leak, everything should be sealed. It is clear that this is not always possible. Yet exclusion must always go hand in hand with responsibility. Solutions should always be part of intermediate steps that have been well thought-through. We would have to render more fruitful the halting problem of computation (a problem in computability theory), and valorize it positively. That an algorithm sometimes arrives at no solution and searches for a solution forever, even though the problem is describable, is certainly perplexing, but it shows that for some problems there is no permanent solution, and that solving the problem too soon and with too much finality only leads to further problems.

While exclusion is to be avoided, interruption, on the other hand, is to be welcomed. Without interruption, there would be no interactivity in computer systems. Processes, operations, algorithms, rules, laws, and agreements in execution must be stoppable and interruptible during their temporal execution so that they can be reflected upon, reviewed, and adjusted and changed accordingly.

5 In a review of *History and Obstinacy*, the North-American Marxist literature scholar Fredric R. Jameson (b. 1934) translated *Eigensinn* as "self-will" (1988a, 158). It could also be translated as "waywardness" or more commonly "obstinacy." The concept of the autonomy of the socialized worker by Italian *operaismo* surely resonates a lot with obstinacy and self-will (see e.g., Negri 1989, 147).

 But exclusion can also occur during interruptions if, for example, not all instances are informed and involved operators are decoupled. This is the case when interaction, interruption, and data input coincide, with the operator barely understanding, registering, or following any of the processes involved in their interaction. Touchscreen interaction data such as touch location, time, and frequency, combined with information regarding the content displayed, is often used to create user profiles, which then enable the targeting of specifically tailored advertising. However, the interaction data extracted here, if commOnized, could be analyzed and used for entirely different, collaborative purposes. If we think of this in terms of property, splitting off this data without consultation with its producers is tantamount to theft or robbery. This is certainly one of the reasons why, as with forests and meadows a few centuries ago, there is talk of enclosure or land grabbing (see e.g., Andrejevic 2007).

Because the exclusion of exclusion alone appears all too normative and could cause intellectual resistance, this procedure must additionally be turned inside out, embedded and mediated in processes of self-organization: Instead of excluding only operations of devaluing, of waste, of destruction, additional media-based methods and operations ought to be found to strengthen and sustain connections. If neoliberalism singles people out, individualizes, isolates and excludes, then commOnism should bring together, solidarize, integrate, and accommodate in an open and adaptive way. Moreover, this involves not only directly implementing concrete networks, modes of operation, algorithms, and thus ultimately institutions, but also modeling them in a computational way. That is, simulating them in a prefigurative fashion, with foresight, and with an experimental design. In dancing, too, the concrete movements must always be mentally imagined and prefigured. For counter-dancing digitality, we would sometimes have to feed our imaginative thinking with new mental choreographies.

Procedures, algorithms, protocols, and laws in execution would have to be made designable as dynamic institutions, incorporating the modes of operation of heterogeneous interactions and forms of exchange. Institutions would have to be imagined less as set, unchanging, architectural structures like the court, the museum, the university, or the market, but rather as dance, as ensemble, as multiscale polyphonic operativity that produces, conditions, and provokes manifold manifestations of *dispositifs* of power. According to German sociologist Robert Seyfert (b. 1975), however, this is not only about the so-called human being:

> Bodily affect, space, and the times of an institution mutually determine each other: the movement of bodies creates institutional temporality and spatiality just as space and the respective time produce bodies. To describe the particular life of an institution, one cannot rely solely on the people within it. (2008, 211, my translation)

This prescient turn of phrase from a sociologist, which dates back to the early 2010s, toward the affective and the more-than-human, i.e., toward assemblages and institutions of animals, plants, environments, but also machines, artifacts, and matter, can be interpreted as an echo of feminist philosopher Donna Haraway's (b. 1944) already classic 1980s works on the cyborg (see 1991) and her later concept of the "critter" (see 2007). Meanwhile, the 2010s were characterized by two further trends, first in terms of the planetary and global warming (for example, the March 11, 2011 earthquake and tsunami disaster in northeastern Japan and the accompanying nuclear disaster in Fukushima) and second to new forms of protest following the 2007–10 global financial crisis and the 2011 Occupy movement. In this context, the then still rather new social networks of communication, expression, and opinion dissemination were initially credited with playing a positive role.

The insight that atmospheres, geospheres, ecospheres, biospheres, semiospheres, and technospheres are intertwined in multiple ways and form institutions that are conditioned, framed, and timed by rules of computation, by algorithms, protocols, rhythms, and fluctuations, was already elaborated in the cultural, media, and social sciences during the 1990s, i.e., in parallel to the previously described work by Ostrom on the commons. The social diffusion of computation in universities, in companies, factories, offices, and even into living rooms and bedrooms, opened up numerous fields of discourse that should not be forgotten. I will take up two of them, synthesize them, and make them dance.

Kurz and Kittler

The discourse production of the Foucault-Kittler network and that of the Marx-Kurz-Meretz connection, like probably many of the discussions of the 1990s, went on for years in parallel universes. It is therefore about time that we couple and modulate them in order to enable a different way of thinking and acting. The antagonist to Friedrich Kittler was not considered to be Robert Kurz, but rather the Frankfurt School under the guidance of Jürgen Habermas (b. 1929). In this context, the discursive hostility probably came more from Kittler, for whom the Habermasian division of "reason" into a communicative reason on the one hand and an instrumental one on the other, was fundamentally wrong. For Kittler, who followed Foucault here, the production of reason, knowledge, culture, and history is always intertwined with materialities and power, bodies, and media, and cannot be viewed in isolation from these entanglements. It is therefore no coincidence that these points of criticism were already formulated in the 1980s in the Foucault-Habermas debate.

Kittler was appointed to the Humboldt-Universität zu Berlin from the Ruhr University Bochum in 1993. At the same time his essay collection *Draculas Vermächtnis* (Dracula's Legacy) proffered a further intensification of his theses, methods, and approaches already elaborated in *Discourse Networks 1800/1900* and *Gramophone, Film, Typewriter*, which flowed into the then-emerging German media studies. In the decades before, he had been one of the first to disseminate the theories of Jacques Lacan (1901–81), Michel Foucault, Gilles Deleuze (1925–95), and Félix Guattari (1930–92) into the German-speaking world. In the 1990s, the work of French theorists slowly began to gain a foothold in German universities as well. So Kittler really had nothing more to fear.

The texts in *Draculas Vermächtnis*, such as "Die Welt des Symbolischen," "Vom Take-Off der Operatoren," "Protected Mode," or "Es gibt keine Software," were already part of the media studies canon by the end of the 1990s and still testify to Kittler's distinctive and detailed technological knowledge of media – both in terms of analog electronics and digital programming, which he elegantly combined and modulated with the aforementioned French theories and their German references, especially Nietzsche and Georg W. F. Hegel (1770–1831), but also with historical agents and the contexts of media, science, and technology and their respective discourses, mostly by excluding Marx and the Frankfurt School. Kittler not only soldered together components and microchips in self-etched copper circuit boards to create highly complicated media dispositifs such as a programmable sound synthesizer as shown by German media scholar Sebastian Döring (b. 1977) and artist Jan-Peter Sonntag (b. 1965), but could also write small programs at the lowest programmable level of a PC using assembly code. Until his untimely death in 2011, he worked with free software and a Linux operating system. It is in this context that his now-famous definition of happiness from the preface of *Gramophone, Film, Typewriter* should be understood:

> Whosoever is able to hear or see the circuits in the synthesized sound of CDs or in the laser storms of a disco finds happiness. A happiness beyond the ice, as Nietzsche would have said. (1999, xli)

To counter-dance digitality we must also learn how we might hear and see the circuits of digital media technology. And in doing so, we must learn to find "happiness" beyond bourgeois-liberalist modernity!

While media scholars associate the 1990s with the spread of the Personal Computer and the Internet, as well as the popularization of cyberspace as a hopeful concept, it should not be forgotten that these years also mark the first years after the triumph of the so-called free market economy and the fall of real socialism. In this context, the outsider Kurz, with *Der Kollaps der Modernisierung* (The Collapse of Modernization), published in 1991, offered the astute and sharp-witted thesis that these events were only the beginning of the end of capitalism. At the time, this was the subject of much ridicule. From the perspective of the 2020s and the global financial crisis of 2007–10, however, his thesis has hardly lost any of its relevance. Kurz not only criticized the market economy, but argued for a "perspective of radical abolition of the modern commodity and its world system." For through the market economy "vital production is stopped without regard to needs," but at the same time life-threatening and profit-oriented enterprises are "pulled through" (1991, 270, my translation). The free market thus brutally fails every day.

Der Kollaps der Modernisierung barely addresses what were then brand-new media technologies – computers and the Internet – but this is quickly atoned for. Already towards the end of the decade, in 1997's *Antiökonomie und Antipolitik – Zur Reformulierung der sozialen Emanzipation nach dem Ende des Marxismus* (Anti-Economy and Anti-Politics – On the Reformulation of Social Emancipation after the End of Marxism), some convincing and momentous conditions and counter-measures for the success of social emancipation projects are proposed, among them the ambitious requirement:

> to develop elements ... of a "microelectronic natural economy" that fundamentally escapes the socialization

principle of value and can no longer be encompassed by it. (Kurz 1997, 73, my translation)

To interpret the emergence of microelectronics, the computer, and planetary networks in a positive light is already unusual for a technology critic, for usually the developments that accompanied them were demonized. Kurz is not only interested in approaches that operate against capitalist technologies – this would be immediately understandable – but he argues quite in the Marxist-Hegelian manner for ways that would rather also synthesize the productivity of microelectronics with the concerns of his radical critique of value and thus "sublate" its capitalist part. No mere instrumentalization of technologies for socialist, non-profit purposes was called for here, but rather the technologies of automation and networking would have to be investigated, appropriated, and reshaped, which would eventually allow their "capitalist artifacts to be critically selected out" (1997, 63). Consequently, the means must be structurally transformed and reprogrammed into counter-agents. Here Kurz remains pragmatic and proposes to start not with production but primarily at the application and usage of microelectronic technologies. He concluded that the "production conditions of chips," the "primary industry and the basic production of microelectronics itself ... are not the cornerstone [or basis] but rather the keystone of transformation" (ibid., 66). Keystones are placed at the very end of the construction; before changing the production at the source, it is more important to focus on "the constitution and development of social spaces of emancipation" (ibid.). For this, it is necessary that we "actively transform the technological potential and experiment with it, that is, for example, develop our own hardware combinations and our own software" (ibid., 67). It is a matter of holding on to the abolition of private and state ownership of the means of production and at the same time striving for a "decoupling of a social space of emancipatory cooperation from commodity exchange, monetary relations, and abstract accounting of services" (ibid., 73). This decoupling would have to take place at the "endpoints" (ibid., 77) of material networking processes, that is, planetary supply chains, and information and data networks. Endpoints are also places of receiving, consumption, application, and use of goods, food, energy, services, information, knowledge, and so on. Simply put, it is about prioritizing use value instead of exchange value, which normally takes priority. Rather, the latter is to be eliminated.

This prefigurative – and for the coming years highly important – intellectual movement, which Kurz articulated as early as 1997, starts at the end: with the suffering, the needy, the consumers, the beneficiaries in order to immediately transform their passivity into an activity that intertwines consumption with production. The needs of planetary ecosystems have to be considered as well. In Kurz's microelectronic natural economy, this entanglement, which is at the same time a mediation, no longer occurs through the economic form of value (see Heinrich 2012, 55; and Franklin 2021, 51), i.e., through monetary pricing of goods, labor, and time, nor through the exchange of goods, but on the basis of needs that desire to be satisfied and the requirements of those involved. The idea is to create a "mediated identity" (Kurz 1997, 88) of producers and consumers. Kurz finds approaches for this in cooperatives or mutual associations, not of commodity production, but ones dedicated to practical use and for users, such as consumer cooperatives, housing cooperatives, and cooperatives such as cultural and educational institutions. These could form networks and jointly transform the planetary, material technosphere from the endpoints sector by sector. Building cooperatives could run sandpits or brick factories, or coffee consumer cooperatives could source coffee from a cooperative in Latin America.

The more complex and the larger the network of these cooperatives, the more critical the mediation between consumers and producers, which operates by "material and technical sharing of tasks" (ibid.) and would have to be programmed and structured in such a way that "the necessary items are produced in the necessary quantity and quality" (ibid). Consequently, we are dealing here with the variant of a specially developed and programmed, decentrally-distributed planned economy that self-organizes through the participation of many.[6] How this mediation should operate in concrete terms is unfortunately not formulated in detail, but there are three important indications to follow.

First, Kurz differentiates between direct mediation, such as through language, and indirect mediation through value. Mediation through language needs to be practiced, tried out, and refined, so that the starting point should first be where the relationship between production and consumption becomes tangible, without "intervening instances" (ibid., 77). So we are dealing here with media in the "in-between." Food producers and consumers who are all in the same place, perhaps a marketplace, could, in my fabulation, "communicate" with each other even without language, but at the same time also without commodity prices, for instance by allowing each consumer to buy a certain number of products from a certain number of producers. Of course, this scenario would not be a variant of sale or exchange of goods, but simply of distribution and mediation. One would have to consider, however, that not all products enjoy the same popularity, but that some would be more, and others less popular. Since the producers have covered their own needs, the goal would be to distribute all surplus food (fruit, vegetables, etc.). Only as much may be taken as can reasonably be consumed, and so on. This is, as was mentioned, in the realm of the fictitious. In order that all participants be satisfied, however, relatively few rules would suffice, which could also be modified. Such rules would first have to be negotiated through language, tried out and, if accepted by all, communicated and practiced. This would then be a direct mediation through language as an embedded medium. An already practiced network of consumers/producers

6 The planned economy remains a topical issue (see Daum and Nuss 2021; also Phillips and Rozworski 2019).

could certainly carry out such a distribution action after a certain time without having to speak. However, the direct mediation with language seems to be more appropriate here, since it is sometimes about more complex situations such as seasonal dynamics and differences in effort when it comes to food production. Language is known to be a complex medium with polysemantic openness. In the case of indirect mediation through value, we now have the special situation that it is no longer a matter of simple distribution, but distribution is indirect, that is, mediated through the exchange of goods and the money relation. Here, food production no longer serves to meet needs within a larger communal network, but is optimized for commodity exchange. This is to be avoided.

Second, in order to build the intended consumer-producer networks in a manner that is as real and proper as possible, the entire material but also affective reproduction of society must be examined both practically and critically, and "a kind of ruthless 'socio-ecological politics of revelation'" (ibid., 100) must be pursued. The point here, I conclude, is not to reduce these processes and try to bring everything down to a common denominator in order to simplify or bring them into line – that would be value measurement for commodity exchange – rather, each of these material and affective processes of social reproduction is to be measured in detail and idiosyncrasies are to be teased out. It is clear that this will not work without a unified, scientific language of description and standards. However, this measurement, technomathematization, and operationalization must under no circumstances serve profit generation. It is important to cultivate increases in complexity and not to focus on simplification, as is done, for example, through the use of monetary forms of value.

In describing his practical-critical method of investigation, Kurz was inspired by the Situationists, who, for their part, investigated socioeconomic landscapes, also called "psychogeographies," by means of walks, observations, the *dérive,* and experimental cartographies, especially in Paris around 1970 (ibid., 101). Since landscapes and cities in the 1990s were already increasingly permeated by microelectronic, i.e., computational and algorithmic spheres and rhythms, it is also no wonder that Kurz emphasizes that the "cybernetic … set of rules" of those spheres would have to be examined in detail, critically and practically, in order to investigate both the planetary interconnectedness of consumer-producer networks as well as to be able to produce forms of cybernetic "subversion" (ibid., 104). This remains topical in terms of the 2020s, as according to the Californian media theorist Benjamin Bratton (b. 1968), today cybernetic control circuits form levels of profit-oriented exploitation machinery, algorithms, protocols, laws, and infrastructures which are layered across the planet, and which he famously called "the stack" (see 2016).

Discourse Potentials

The fact that the opportunities offered by Kurz's approaches and theories of *Antiökonomie und Antipolitik* are still being discussed 30 years later is probably a credit to the critical computer scientist Stefan Meretz (b. 1962), who strongly influenced the free software movement in Germany. As early as 1999, Meretz further extended Kurz's transformation theory with value critique as a core method through the concept of "seed form" (see Meretz 2001, 2003), expanding it with approaches and concepts from the German Critical Psychology of Klaus Holzkamp (1927–95). The concept of the seed form was sometimes taken up in the discourse network of the Oekonux movement which formed around the turn of the millennium, but it seems not to have been used for a long time. It is no coincidence that *Linux und Co.*, published in 2000 and which until a few years ago had been Meretz's most successful book, leaves out the seed form and relies instead on an extremely simple model in which the productive forces have three stages of development that build on each other in a linear fashion. The optimism associated with this, which Meretz later dispensed a little more evenly, was criticized above all by allies such as Sabine Nuss (b. 1967) and Michael Heinrich (b. 1957) (see e.g., Nuss and Heinrich 2002). Together with Ernst Lohoff (b. 1960), Norbert Trenkle (b. 1959), and Hans Jürgen Krysmanski (1936–2016), Nuss and Heinrich took part in the first Oekonux conference in Dortmund in April 2001. Dutch media scholar and Internet activist Geert Lovink (b. 1959) was an early observer of this movement (see 2003, 157). There is also an audio recording on archive.org of an interview Lovink conducted with Kurz from the 1990s.

The common intention of this mainly German Oekonux discourse network was to link the conception of economics and Linux, with the goal of establishing, also "offline," the positive principles and effects of the free software culture, those that Benkler later pertinently described. This did not go unnoticed by members of what was then the emerging generation of German media scholars, such as Volker Grassmuck (b. 1961) and Inke Arns (b. 1968). Grassmuck had at that time been organizing the Wizard of OS conferences. The first one took place in July 1999 in the Haus der Kulturen der Welt with the participation of scholars such as Wolfgang Hagen (1950–2022), Armin Medosch (1962–2017), and also Kittler. Later participants included Florian Cramer (b. 1969) and Felix Stalder (b. 1968). Meretz took part in the fourth and final conference in 2006.

In 2002, Grassmuck also wrote *Freie Software – Zwischen Privat- und Gemeineigentum* (Free Software – Between Private and Public Property), an introduction to free software published in collaboration with the Bundeszentrale für politische Bildung (Federal Agency for Civic Education), and was one of the first to discuss the Oekonux movement in terms of media studies. Yet, although Grassmuck studied at the Free University of Berlin in the 1980s and contributed to the autonomist journal *radikal*, there is no reference in *Freie Software* to Marx, to the "old" Frankfurt School of Theodor W. Adorno (1903–69), or to Italian *operaismo* (workerism). While his exposition of the (intellectual) commons with reference to Ostrom and her concepts is convincing (see

Grassmuck 2002, 406–07), the derivation of the history of the commons lacks references to concepts such as primitive accumulation. While there is talk of "closure" in the sense coined by Max Weber (1864–1920), there is a lack of clear statements and critical potential. This shows how outdated and marginal the critical Marxist discourses around Kurz and Meretz were, especially in the early 2000s. Most of that generation, especially in Germany, must have been reluctant to dig out and revitalize the Marxist sins of their youth.

While Marxism became part of syllabi in media studies and related disciplines again no later than 10 years after 1989, exemplified by *Cyber-Marx,* a 1999 classic by Canadian media scholar Nick Dyer-Witheford (b. 1951), its rehabilitation in the German-speaking world was somewhat slower.[7] It was mainly driven by Jens Schröter (b. 1970), Leander Scholz (b. 1969), and Oliver Marchart (b. 1968). Although Marchart is not a media scholar, but a political philosopher and sociologist, a look at his academic curriculum vitae around 2000 shows that he was deeply committed to approaches from technologies and media studies during those years. The mediation of German media studies and Marxism often went via post-structuralists such as Félix Guattari, Gilles Deleuze, or Jacques Derrida (1930–2004).

The turn of the century was also the time when German media studies, especially the discourse inspired by Kittler, first had to establish itself as a university discipline with professorships in Weimar, Basel, Berlin, and Bochum, before forming alliances with other discourses, which in turn took several years. Not coincidentally, Marx-Kittler syntheses were thus only achieved in the late 2010s by the aforementioned media scholar Schröter in collaboration with Swiss-German media scholar Till A. Heilmann (b. 1974). Not without some irony, the two presented their

7 Dyer-Witheford was pertinent for taking up the topic of the commons into media studies. Italian feminist and Marxist media scholar Tiziana Terranova (b. 1967) gave this direction a further spin (see 2004; 2022, 26–41).

groundbreaking program of "neo-critical media studies" in the very year when, for the first time, the three top-listed companies globally in terms of turnover via stock market value consisted solely of companies from the digital industry: Apple, Alphabet (formerly Google), and Microsoft (see Schröter and Heilmann 2016). 2016 was also the year of the Brexit referendum, and in November a right-wing conservative, misogynistic neoliberal was elected president of the United States. In both cases, the social networking infrastructure played a significant role in attracting and radicalizing voters. In 2013, we learned from former CIA employee and NSA contractor Edward Snowden (b. 1983) that our online activities and emails are monitored worldwide by the intelligence agencies of the superpowers. Since 2016, we have known that powerful groups and their networks can use targeted algorithmic manipulation on social media to influence not only consumer behavior, but also the political attitudes and agency of the population in a way that strongly influences society.

While the crisis of the liberal middle classes, the crumbling of their worldviews, and the urgency of systemic change in the face of global warming gave rise to the Marx-Kittler synthesis, the global financial crisis of 2007–08 and the European debt crisis of 2009–10 were already catalyzing the widespread adoption of commoning. In late 2009, Ostrom received the Nobel Prize in Economics for her theory of the commons. In the course of this, the commoning principle was mixed with many approaches not only from the free software movement, the Oekonux network, and peer production, but was also taken up in the discourse on art, architecture, and urbanism, and by Marxist thinkers such as Silvia Federici, Hans Widmer (b. 1947), and George Caffentzis (b. 1945). They knew each other through the Midnight Notes Collective, which formed in New York in the late 1970s, and have been in contact ever since.

In the German-speaking world, Silke Helfrich (1967–2021) played the role of initiator, and spread commoning in wide circles, at first following Ostrom, but then later adapted, modulated, and transformed through her own work (see 2007, 2015, 2019). Her glorious idea of describing commoning as the organization, choreography, and interplay of various interlocking "patterns," and its further development by Marcus Meindel and the Global Commoning System, also becomes operative for counter-dancing digitality.

Anacrusis

CommOnistic cooperativity (CoC), to sum up what has been elaborated so far, consists of operations that, first, preserve the commons as a form of solidarity, while proactively serving the ecosocial fulfillment of needs. Second, CoC is characterized by a connection, mediation, and networking of productivity and consumption. And third, it is not linked to the exchange of goods by means of monetary mediation through the free market – what is produced should be made use of. It is not intended for sale and commodity exchange; at best it is only for a utilitarian exchange. CoC, fourth, largely excludes the exclusion of any part of an always-open world, both with living and non-living entities. Fifth, this means that much would be accessible to many and that private property would be greatly reduced. Sixth, CoC allows temporary exclusions, but only with the goal of re-inclusion, with commitment and responsibility. The raw materials of the "private" toothbrush can later become useful in other forms, do not become waste, and thus do not disappear from the network of relationships. Seventh (and last, for the time being), it is essential for CoC to grasp, uncover, and understand the fabric, networks, and interweaving of planetary dispositifs and logistics. CoC cannot become operational without critical media, and the humanities-driven and social science approaches that accompany the technologically and scientifically implemented transformation. Thus, it is crucial to understand CoC as a social and at the same time medial practice.

According to German cultural sociologist Andreas Reckwitz (b. 1970), a social practice entails "routinized bodily activities; as ... behavioral acts they are movements of the body. A social practice is the product of training the body in a certain way" (2002, 251). It "consists of certain bodily and certain mental activities" (ibid., 252). Social practices can thus also be seen as dance. Reckwitz's practice theory is also informed by media theory and acknowledges that "subject–subject relations cannot claim any priority over subject–object relations, as far as the production and reproductions of social order(liness) is concerned" (ibid., 253). Still, social practices are also practices of mediation and it is important to study the co-operativity involved. This media oblivion when it comes to sociological approaches is to be countered by the perspective of medial operations and their rhythms as a sub-unit of social practices. Counter-dancing digitality thus becomes graspable only as a practice of sociality and mediality.

Canadian media scholar Wendy Hui Kyong Chun (b. 1969) looks at the operativities in digital capitalism from the perspective of behaviors and habitual patterns. In her astute diagnosis of ubiquitous social networks, she exposes not only their polarizing effects but, more importantly, makes the underlying principle of homophily comprehensible, which she situates in terms of media history in the context of quantitative social science and network analysis inspired by graph theory. Social media reinforces our preference for sameness by always only showing us information that matches our own biases. Their algorithm-driven offerings, which they provide via the "feed," thus smother any existing preference and interest for otherness. In this, Chun criticizes the way that racism on the net is thereby trivialized to simply being an unavoidable effect of an inherently benign preference and pleads "to think ... through the generative power of discomfort" and to imagine and create "different, more inhabitable, patterns" (2018, 89). In this sense, it is important to advocate for diversity and anti-homophily as key principles within the social and media practices of a commOnist cooperativity.

German Marxist feminist Bini Adamczak (b. 1979) argues similarly to Chun, making a strong case for the notion of relationality. Since only the shifting and modulating of relations (see 2017, 245) could make social transformation possible, she argues for solidarity-oriented modes of relating through "synapses and switching points" (ibid., 263, my translation), which at the same time would also have to prove capable of conflict (see ibid., 274). In doing so, Adamczak emphasizes that solidarity "is not a question of attitude [but] a question of relation. Not, how should I behave toward the others, but, in what relationship do we want to put ourselves?" (Ibid., 270, my translation) For the focus on attitude alone is, I conclude, an overly bourgeois-liberal and individualistic mindset. Rather, it must be assumed that we are always situated in a network of relationships anyway, and that this makes it much more important to cultivate the connection, the interaction, and the relation as a whole, and thus to regard it as part of a dance.

The success of a commOnistic cooperativity (CoC) depends significantly on the mediation between the interpersonal and transpersonal levels. To put it in vulgar sociological terms, it is about the entanglement of community and society. This is the core idea of the seed form theory as formulated by Meretz and Sutterlütti in *Kapitalismus aufheben* (*Make Capitalism History, 2018/2022)*. It is at the same time both a theory of sublation and of liberation. Commoning is defined here as "a social relationship based on voluntariness and collective disposal, generating a logic of inclusion and leading to inclusive conditions" (148). Based on the concept of the seed form, which Meretz had already articulated at the turn of the millennium, the pair developed theoretical building blocks highly relevant to counter-dancing digitality that aim for a "process of trial and error" (79). Following Adamczak, their "possibility utopia" (93) is a "utopia of relationships" (102) which both emphasizes the solidarity-oriented mediation and fulfillment of needs and, following the German

 Critical Psychology of Holzkamp, establishes the sociality of human beings in an evolutionary way (see 115).

The seed form theory is an approach on how an alternative form of society could develop from an already existing one, in order to eventually abolish it. Based on certain preconditions, resistance to the existing social structure develops from a seed form. At some point, a pressure to change arises. Crises operate in a catalyzing way here. They might provoke a widespread need for functional change. The seed form establishes itself. This leads to a change in dominance. The transformation is complete. The interpersonal seed form has become the transpersonal elementary form. It now permeates the entire network (see 207).

The basic principle of the seed form theory is that all parties have a solidarity-oriented, networked capacity for action. Based on this, transpersonal and unconditional "inclusion relationships" (122) provide the basis for an "inclusive society" (136). This is not only about the satisfaction of material existential needs, but also about the satisfaction of symbolic and social needs, which then also affects the diversity of means and media practices (see 127). The question of prioritization of needs is not solved in this process, because resource limitations create conflicts (see 152, 166). Planet Earth also has needs that must be taken into account as well. In principle, however, the needs would first have to be satisfied in an evenly distributed manner, so that no major inequalities can occur. In addition, there is the following idea:

> Generally speaking, commonism dissolves the contradiction between my needs and those of others. Crucially, difference and conflicts remain, but I am actually better off if others are better off. (181)

In order for a network of relationship conditions and relations of need to achieve an overall social scope, not only does the overall social recognition of the necessity of alternative social practice become critical, but the transformation of the seed form into an elemental form must also be concretely achievable. To this end, the social practice of mediation must be pushed into view. Meretz and Sutterlütti articulate this as follows:

> Direct relationships are exceeded by the fact that they take place via means, therefore indirectly or mediately. Relationships via means connect people unknown to each other in a global net of cooperation. (128–29)

Since means are also media, mediation must be recognized not only as a social practice, but at the same time as a media practice. Media studies and media theoretical perspectives in particular can contribute to the conceptualization, planning, and design of the operativity and technicality of reciprocity-based, transpersonal, and unconditional mediation of relations of inclusion. Presumably, the collaboration between commOnist-inspired activists and sympathetic programmers, engineers, designers, and tinkerers would be possible without media scholars, but the latter could play a helpful and mediating role when it comes, for example, to the question of how we can experience transpersonal cooperation "with our senses" (133). Here, insights, approaches, and experiments from the history of media aesthetics and art could help. This book intends to show that this would only be the beginning.

In *Make Capitalism History*, networks of relations and needs (both of the people and of the Earth), and of consumers and producers, are sensibly also referred to as commons (see 163). This allows not only the switching of perspectives between micro- and macro-levels, but also a recursive, fractal movement through the levels. Not only are resources commons, but so are the networks that share, use, and manage resources in a solidarity-oriented and cooperative manner. CommOnistic cooperativities thus become commons that could intertwine with other commons, multiscalar through several levels up to the planetary level. Conversely, in microstructural terms, a commons consists of a relationship, a non-trivial connection, through which operations of cooperation and organization occur. Thus, the relationship itself becomes a commons whose basic operation is transmission.

The German media philosopher Sybille Krämer (b. 1951) has pertinently dealt with the manifold media theoretical semantics, concepts, and perspectives of transmission (see 2015). Meanwhile, the German media scholar Georg Christoph Tholen (b. 1948), whose lectures I eagerly attended as a student in Basel, assigned to transmission the most extensive media theoretical significance. According to Tholen, storage is also a transmission that lasts over a longer period of time. And storage combined with transmission forms the basic operations for processing and computation. This is where Krämer's media theory comes in, which is sometimes also a theory of mediation. It describes transmission from the point of view of embodied materialization and temporalization with a narrow focus on the mediator, the bearer of the message, the messenger, the carrier pigeon, the scroll, or the telegram. The relation between two entities here becomes "a figuration of the third" (Krämer 2015, 82), that is, the third agency that forms the relation between two instances, such as people: "The messenger," Krämer argues, "is not in command of his speech, and it is not surprising that in his function as a transmitter he can also be easily replaced with non-human entities" (ibid., 85).

How would a message transmission network operate that does not instrumentalize the messenger as usual, but in which the content of the message is co-determined, filtered, interpreted, and explained by the carrier medium? For the commOnistic cooperativity this would have the consequence that the message expressing need, provided with date and location, could be transformed immediately by a messenger who is sufficiently willful into a search for the potential means to satisfy need, with the message returning immediately to the sender upon successfully finding a recipient who is, for example, a food producer. Such an algorithmically-implemented system would certainly be one of the basic structures of a larger CoC-based society.

Meretz and Sutterlütti describe their vision and version of a commOnistic cooperativity with reference to "stigmergy" (2022, 160), a concept from zoology and termite research that later found its way into the field of knowledge of emergence within complexity science. Also known as swarm research, it opens up a constructive field of interference between political self-determining self-organization, and self-organization from the perspective of technoscience and the natural sciences.

The word stigmergy is formed from the ancient Greek terms stigmata and ergon. Stigmata are stitches, wounds, or burn marks. The negative connotation is often overlooked and masked with the term "marking."[8] This deliberate and hopefully liberating marking and tracing could be interpreted, in Krämer's words, as an "inversion of the messenger's errand" (2015, 175). Here, the message is "found," read, and decoded by the receiver. Ergon, in turn, means work, i.e., operativity. The message works. Stigmergy offers a perspective from below based on operations and operator. It is often assumed that the operations when combined as a whole system generate an added value that exceeds a single operation alone. However, the fact that this is always normative, definitional, value-creating, often discriminatory, or preservationist thinking that is no longer tenable is often not reflected. The opposite can easily be argued. For there are simply more individual operations, which together can result in an almost infinite variety of total operation. Accordingly, the above-mentioned description of a commons consisting of further sub-commons is helpful only under the condition that these commons are always open, inclusive, and dynamically mutable. The same is true for the operations and operators that make the commons possible.

8 There surely is a critical history of markings into human bodies resonating here. Following such a path into the deep history of slavery is a scholarly learning I have just recently started to investigate.

Operators are also called agents in technoscientific jargon, especially when self-organization is simulated in computer models, that is, programmed into algorithms. This will be discussed in detail in the second part of this book. CommOnistic stigmergy means a self-organized, volunteer-based, decentralized system that, through its activity, yields a relational network of symbolic messages about needs and helps to meet them by utilizing various means of satisfying them. Meretz and Sutterlütti emphasize the importance of these messages not having one-dimensional, purely quantitative properties, but rather that they are multidimensional and qualitatively structured (see 2022, 161), otherwise there is a danger that the whole closely approaches a market mechanism based on price signals. Decentralized networks already exist in multiple implementations, but they function only because the addressees (in the simplest case it would be two), are already defined and the message must "merely" be transferred from A to B. Within a commOnistic cooperativity of commons, however, first of all the needs would have to be carefully determined, which could be simplified as a "channel search," in order to find the corresponding productive entities, which could then satisfy these needs as recipients. Only then can a relationship between producers and consumers get established through mediation. There would be a need, for each commons, for the following to be defined, negotiated, and planned in detail: how this mediation takes place in technological, material, and spatiotemporal terms and what it includes; whether only the information is transmitted or the products are transported right away; how the content and form structure of the message are programmed; whether the mediation takes place before, during, or after the production; and how the production processes are organized, distributed, and planned. Here the only point is to suggest that this would be possible and that it is a question of framework conditions. First the potential of a commOnistic cooperativity has to be recognized, in order to concretize it step by step in each case with the help of some basic principles, which Helfrich also called patterns. How all this could be thought of and practiced as dance, and what insights could be gained from this thought exercise, will be elaborated in the following chapter.

[2]

Counter-Dance

Dancing is neither pure instinct, nor a purely machine-like, vegetative, isolated algorithm, and certainly not context-free. Dancing needs to be learned and oscillates between the affective-somatic unconscious and collective common sense. If we hand ourselves over directly to the affects, especially those of the dispositifs dominated by profit-oriented powers and operativities, we suffer only spontaneous convulsions, catastrophes, disruptions, or network collapses. If, on the other hand, we are prepared to process the affects and to learn how to deal with them, in order to then react with our own attitudes, then this would correspond to a dance. In this process, the learning and sublimation phase can be relatively short and simple, as in a techno rave, but our ability to learn is its condition. Dancing is learning, and has less to do with anger, struggle, insurrection (or more generally speaking, aggression), and more to do with endurance, attitude, elegance, skill, insight, resistance, and art. A dance does not move within a pre-programmed framework, otherwise it would simply be an exercise in repetition, foot drill, if you will. Nevertheless, dancing is not based on spontaneity alone. Rhythms and rules must be observed, patterns generated and learned. A dance is always open, adaptive, responsive to the environment around it, and changeable. Dance can thus oppose and tackle foot drill, make it fugitive, and then liquefy it. Dancing can accordingly elude pure control and thus commodification.

Dancing, I suggest, forms an adequate antidote to confront the inhuman, the non-human digitality and its technological enclosures and land grabs that arise in the name of commodifying and exploiting everything mundane, and to suspend and sublate it in something better.

Algorithms can also be danced. CommOnistic cooperativity can be danced as a counter-dance. This is less a metaphor, but rather meant literally. We must confront capitalist digitality as an artificial and inhuman structure in an artistic way, that is, as a dance: first, neither purely affective nor purely discursive, but both at the same time, and second, with simulation-modeling, automatic-fictionalization, imagining, dreaming, and designing operativities, and as an affective-technological structure of the counter-algorhythmic. For this, an attitude is a condition in which technomathematics, algorithmics, and rhythmics – i.e., the abstract-symbolic, the material in space-time, and the living – come together and dance with each other. Digitality operating within the framework of a commOnistic cooperativity would have to come alive *and* at the same time become artistic and poetic, prefiguratively anticipatory, and future-oriented. I propose that this dual approach is of importance for all of our futures. The signaling pathway leading to counter-dancing must first of all go through the process of looking more closely into our bodies and the research field of neurophysiology.

The Affective Somatic

"Affects dwell at the transitions, they guard the interval – guarding against closure" (2022, 39). Austrian-German feminist media scholar Marie-Luise Angerer (b. 1958) poetically describes the transition zones between physiological perception and cognitive consciousness. What is relevant for dance is her thought that "rather than coinciding fully with the movement of the psycho-organic, the timing of the machine organizes the membrane between inside and outside by means of the movement of the affective" (78), while noting that disturbances and delays can still occur in this process.

In Brian Massumi's (b. 1956) *The Autonomy of Affect* (1995), the North American philosopher, translator of Deleuze-Guattari, and one of the initiators of post-structuralist affect theory, distinguished emotion and affect in the way that emotions can be described sociolinguistically, but affects are experienced subdiscursively as rhythmic change of intensities. Because emotions are linguistically describable, they would be property, whereas affects would be indescribable, unpossessable, and thus in a sense expropriated (see 88), a sort of commons I would say. Affects are difficult to recognize and control. They are fugitive and, understood in this way, have a willfulness and obstinacy that at the same time offers an opening to the environment. Only with the help of media technologies that can store and measure subliminal nerve signals and other processes in the body would affects become describable and ultimately examinable.

The affective-somatic ends up forming the undercurrent of a social cooperativity, a "social poetics" that the Black Studies activists and writers Fred Moten (b. 1962) and Stefano Harney (b. 1962) call "undercommons," meaning a process "where inseparable differences are continually made" (Moten 2016, 24). This involves structuring "a sociality centered on the invaluable, rather than a political economy absolutely predicated on values" (ibid., 32–33). Undercommons refers to an underground critique, such as that of the university, that does not take apart, isolate, and professionalize, but rather brings together and generates solidarity. A somewhat "clandestine labor" (Harney and Moten 2013, 29), which also operates in subliminal, affective-somatic networks.

The scientific foundations for Massumi's theory of affect are obscured, at least in the version published in 1995. They have also been controversial (see Leys 2011). In this early article the reference to North American neurophysiologist Benjamin Libet (1916–2007) wrongly points to the year 1964 instead of 1994 due to a typo. The given reference at that time was an article by North American science journalist John Horgan (b. 1953) in *Scientific American* mentioning Libet's work (see Horgan 1994, 92). It is only in the 2000s that Massumi provides a proper source that leads to Libet's research from the early 1980s, which in turn points to older experiments conducted in the 1960s and 1970s (see Libet 1985). The liaison of neurophysiology and an emerging theory of affect through Massumi's reception of Libet's experiments prompted German media scholar and Guattari expert Henning Schmidgen (b. 1965) to turn his attention to the history of these "brain-time experiments" and their "research machinery" (see 2014a, 21–22). He was concerned with the science history of time relations, delays, readiness potentials, and sensorimotoric and neurophysiological signals in human bodies and brains.

The affective-somatic is full of rhythms. This was already explored in experiments by the German physiologist Hermann von Helmholtz (1821–94) around 1850:

> A very light electric shock is applied to any part of a human's skin, and the person is instructed, when feeling the shock, to make a certain movement with the hand or teeth as quickly as he can, by which the time-measuring current is interrupted. (1850, 187, my translation)

The delay and travel times of a bio-electric signal in the human body and nervous system were determined by Helmholtz to range from 125 to 200 milliseconds (see ibid., 186; Schmidgen 2014b, 139). Experimental systems to measure the timing of neural signals have been an integral part of neurophysiology ever since. About 100 years later, in the heyday of EEG-based[1] brain research utilizing analog electronic equipment (i.e., magnetic tape data storage), German neuroscientist Hans Helmut Kornhuber (1928–2009) and Austrian-German neuroscientist Lüder Deecke (b. 1938) succeeded in measuring an electrophysiological phenomenon of the brain, which they called the readiness potential. The neurophysiological foundations for Massumi's theory of affect that Libet provided are therefore discourse effects of a history of media and knowledge of neurological experimental systems that is more than 100 years older than, and at times intertwined with, the history of cybernetics. Libet studied, for example, with the North American physiologist Ralph W. Gerard (1900–74), who was a member of the core group involved in the Macy conferences (see Schmidgen 2014a, 433).

In the early 1980s, Libet brought about a curious renaissance regarding the question of subjective and free will, which many physiologists had not dared to ask for some time. Libet's research machinery was still concerned with the question of signal traveling times, but now with emphasis on the conscious, subjective recognition of a "spontaneous" hand movement: The test measurements showed that readiness potentials became measurable first and foremost in the EEG. After an average of 300 milliseconds, the subjects memorized the point of time of their spontaneous hand movement, which they were asked to determine visually by means of a computer-controlled clock. At last, after another 200 milliseconds on average, the hand movement became measurable. It took a total of 500 milliseconds from the readiness potential to the hand movement, and in between

1 EEG = electroencephalography. For a pertinent media history of EEG, see Borck 2018.

 was the time in which the subjects remembered spontaneously having moved their hand (see ibid., 19).

Libet pursued the question of how a spontaneous voluntary action arises in the brain and reintroduced the test subject's subjective judgment as a measurement. He assumed that if a conscious intention or decision initiates a voluntary action, it must precede or at least occur simultaneously with the corresponding neural-cerebral processes as a subjective experience of that intention or decision. Libet's experiment showed the opposite: a voluntarily performed, spontaneous hand movement can be initiated by unconscious brain processes (readiness potential), even before this hand movement becomes noticeable (see 1985, 529). His article was supplemented by numerous comments from neurologists, physiologists, and psychologists; indeed, the length of said commentary was more than double that of Libet's actual study.

While the measurement results were not criticized by most of his fellow scientists, it was mainly Libet's implications that became the subject of critical discourse and controversy. In this instance, self-observation and subjective memory would not be adequate methods for neurophysiological findings. The distinction between conscious and unconscious experiences was deemed outdated. Many motor processes run quasi-automatically and unconsciously after they have been learned. A generalization was considered impossible because different modes of perception had different signal traveling times. The German neurophysiologist Richard Jung (1911–86) commented:

> I agree with Libet that the conscious will mainly selects and controls our action and that unconscious preparatory cerebral mechanisms are important. I doubt Libet's assertion, however, that the subject's will does not consciously initiate specific voluntary acts. (Libet 1985, open peer commentary, 544)

The Finnish neurologist Risto Näätänen (b. 1939) added accordingly that it was questionable to try to measure isolated forms of spontaneity. After all, the test participants would have been instructed beforehand to perform hand movements, and thus they would have had to consciously adjust to them. Therefore, it would only be about the timing of individual movements, which, however, are not to be considered completely isolated. Here perhaps Libet's latent bourgeois-liberal episteme and ethics manifested themselves, because why should it be so important to want to scientifically substantiate spontaneity and positivistic freedom of command in the sense of a liberal-bourgeois "just do it" mentality? If even a twitch cannot be produced fully spontaneously and merely out of "free" will, then this shows how important the cautious and thorough learning of a dance of solidarity in everyday life becomes. This dance would specifically not consist of revolutionary twitches, but rather of a well-considered, laboriously trained, but adaptively transformable organization and operativity, and which would at the same time always be open to the unconscious and the affective-somatic. That Massumi, as a former environmental and anti-nuclear activist and critic of liberalism, was interested in these experiments is probably only due to the fact that the question of free will was experiencing broad popular interest and it was only through this that Libet's experiments became known to him. Here it may be useful to consider the criticism formulated 15 years later by the North American historian of science Ruth Leys (b. 1939), where she accuses Massumi of strictly separating affect and ideology (see 2011, 450); this was of course based on a misunderstanding. Affect according to Massumi is autonomous in the sense that it first spreads imperceptibly in the body of single individuals, but also in groups and as a movement (see 1995, 96), and at the same time can influence ideologies (see ibid., 102). Accordingly, the end of *The Autonomy of Affect* reads:

> The ability of affect to produce an economic effect more swiftly and surely than economics itself means that

> affect is itself a real condition, an intrinsic variable of the late-capitalist system, as infrastructural as a factory. Actually, it is beyond infrastructural, it is everywhere, in effect. ... It is transversal. This ... needs to be taken seriously into account in cultural and political theory. Don't forget. (Ibid., 106)

The rumblings in the underground of the obviously accessible, that is, in the affective-somatic, must be taken seriously because without resistance to the enormous waves and unbearable noise of affect production of profit-oriented dispositifs and corporate networks, we are quickly modulated and transformed by them. CommOnistic cooperativity must therefore already, in the affective-somatic, in the underground of fugitive signals, begin and become operative. This leads to unexpected sources of inspiration, such as the fields of "learning" and "cognition."

Learning to Dance

Moten and Harney refer to the danger of affective-somatic contagion as synaptic work. A mode of work that not only obeys and follows the beats of the profit-driven colonial algorhythm[2] and the compulsion of "logistic capitalism," but also enhances and optimizes it (see 2021, 56). While Moten and Harney do not misspell the word algorithm – they seem to leave that to me – they articulate the logic of the factual constraint of automatic accumulation of capital, M-C-M+, as a 500-year-old rhythm

2 Algorhythm as a term originated from the synthesis of the technomathematical term "algorithm," which is more associated with abstraction and computation, and the musical and sonic term "rhythm," which has more connotations of flow, the real, and the living. At the same time, the cacography algorhythm is tied to alphanumeric notation. As with Derridean différance, the difference between algorithm and algorhythm is inaudible when it is spoken (see Miyazaki 2013). Rhythm as an epistemic filter for a critique of power gradients was already recognized by the French Marxist and later urban sociologist Henri Lefebvre (1901–91), who argued for rhythm analysis as an approach to temporally capture the operativity of a city (see 2004).

accelerated by the algorithm of digital codes they call "zero-one/one-two" and set against it the "algoriddim." *Riddim* in Jamaican dance music means the non-vocal backing of a song. Accordingly, algoriddim means the underground of algorithmic rhythms, but in the sense of a counter-dance, as "contact improvisational violence to the zero-one/one-two, a disruption of its protocols" (ibid., 58). Algoriddim is supposed to make the protocols of Bratton's "stack" and thus the unreasonable operativity of profit-oriented systems dance! But what is the promising operativity that the algoriddim offers as a counter-dance?

Roughly speaking, dancing is about the mediation of subject and environment (see Brown, Martinez, and Parsons 2006, 1157), which simultaneously generates body knowledge. Dancing is a bioelectrical signaling encompassing multiple brain regions. Portuguese dancer and dance scientist Cecília de Lima Teixeira attributes to dancing an intensified proprioceptive capacity that becomes a "central, coordinating tool of self-consciousness" (Lima 2013, 23). Neuroscientist Julia F. Christensen defines dancing as maintaining our psychobiological and mental health with clear positive effects such as the release of rewarding neurotransmitters (endorphins, opioids) that increase immune reactivity (see Christensen, Cela-Conde, and Gomila 2017, 9). The promotion of playful imagination, the ability to learn, communication skills, and the increase in self-observation and self-control of the affective-somatic and social cohesion would be other positive aspects of dancing (see ibid., 16). In contrast, there would definitely also be negative effects such as physical exhaustion, possible injuries, high caloric demand, or inattention to danger (see ibid., 15), but the positive effects outweigh the negative, because otherwise ancient *Homo sapiens* would have long ago abandoned dancing as a practice and ritual.

Dancing forms a cooperative action that produces an intercorporality (see Brown 2022, 3), a social, learning-based, and solidarity-based assemblage of movements. For German dance scholar and political theorist Gabriele Klein (b. 1957), dance practices are:

> critical in the sense that they test new forms of community, friendship, and complicity, as well as experiment with new forms of production. These experimentally structured spaces of experience are also, in a different light, fields for experimenting with alternative social practices. (2013, 139–40)

Klein describes dance as experimenting, practicing, and exercising alternatives, therefore it is also a practice of modeling different futures. Dancing involves a polyphonic ensemble of bodies (human beings, sound bodies), voices, vibrations, moods, and movements. Canadian philosopher and dance scholar Erin Manning (b. 1969) formulated that:

> Despite appearances, movement is not of a body. It cuts across, co-composing with different velocities of movement-moving. It bodies. (2012, 14)

The idea of "movement-moving" comes very close to signaling, waving, and vibrating. Taken this way, dancing is the embodied timing of neurophysiological signals through bodies. Micro-movements and micro-perceptions happen, according to Manning, "through not just the composing body but also the vibrating space of thought" (ibid., 15). In dancing, not only does the body compose, but a vibrating space of thought emerges that informs and couples form and force (see ibid., 20).

The research field of motor learning is concerned with the neurophysiological processes at play in learning motion sequences. According to a neuroscience review paper, motor learning consists of a combination of the implicit, i.e., affective-somatic, unconscious procedures; and the explicit, i.e., learning which can be linguistically and symbolically explained. Explicit instructions, rules, and patterns play an important role especially for learning new movements that later happen in an internalized and quasi-automatic fashion:

> Even if the endpoint of learning is an implicit, procedural skill, the process of arriving at that skill is, in most cases, a richly cognitive enterprise, building on instruction, imitation, and moments of insight. (Krakauer et al. 2019, 616).

In dance, it is both linguistic and non-linguistic cues (sound, tactility/haptics, light, etc.) and body movements that can impact the learning process. And often the goal here would be to internalize the learned process into an automatic process. While explicit, external semantic signals are interruptive and reflective, implicit, affective-somatic signals seem more likely to provide synthesizing effects and mental automation.

Sensorimotor synchronization, i.e., the coordination of rhythmic body movements with an external beat (see Repp and Su 2013, 403), also called sense of rhythm, provides a pertinent example: As evidenced by numerous experiments and studies, anticipation errors of up to 50 milliseconds are observable in human finger tapping with a metronome (see ibid., 406). That is, without practice, humans tend to want to tap faster and faster in such experimental setups. Professional musicians, however, manage to tap steadily without anticipation errors through many years of learning. Unlearned dancing quickly gets lost in a positive feedback loop, whose end becomes an issue of stamina and energy. Learned dancing shows itself in self-control and the use of interruption, and knows how to play with such effects.

Dancing, furthermore, is one of the best examples of the interplay of motor skills and memory, of awareness and action, of perception and prediction. Especially for learning to dance, pattern recognition, i.e., gathering knowledge in combination with body movements, is more successful than fully passively gathering knowledge entirely without motions. The coupling of perception and action in learning processes in brain and body is not only fundamental for learning motor skills, but also for speech and language abilities (see Pulvermüller and Fadiga 2010). According to recent findings in cognitive sciences, prediction also plays an important part in this.

Practicing the Future

Andy Clark (b. 1957), a British neurophilosopher and member of the British Academy, describes perception not as a passive but as an active, generative act in which new sensory signals are responded to with predictions based on sensory experiences that have been accumulated prior (see 2016, 6).

> At the heart of the process lies a probabilistic generative model that progressively alters so as better to predict the plays of sensory data that impinge upon a biological organism or artificial agent. (Ibid., 270)

Sophisticated generative models are at play in perceptual and motor prediction that are constantly updated proactively – this is called "active inference." Here categorical boundaries between nerve signals of command and those of prediction get blurred (see Adams, Shipp, and Friston 2013). Because this approach itself in turn builds a descriptive model, it oscillates as a model between biological organisms and artificial agents.

It is therefore no wonder that German media, theater, and dance scholar Martina Leeker (b. 1959) showed that for several decades, most recently through the work of choreographer Wayne McGregor (b. 1970) in the 2000s, the cognitive sciences and neurophysiology have been short-circuited with dance. Leeker notes that McGregor, together with his fellow dancers, carried out modeling *in actu*, effectively with and through the living bodies of the people involved, and based on the things around them and technical factors (see Leeker 2013, 112). Dancing in such a constellation was modeling carried out in space-time. Accordingly, the idea of automatism experienced a positive reevaluation when viewed from the perspective of dancing (see ibid., 113). To put it simply, learned, generative, and affective-somatic forms of automatism, which the dancer trained through hard work to manifest as habits, were thereby equated with the algorhythmic automatism of digital software modeling. With this juxtaposition, but also synthesis, of a group of learning and practicing dancers as human agents on the one hand and software systems with algorithmic agents on the other, dancing unfortunately also becomes the ideal domain for neoliberal experiments with programmable agents aiming for the "production of a cognitively-optimized environment" (ibid, 119, my translation).

In dancing, multilayered, multimodal, and multitemporal models of reception, prediction, and action emerge in brain and body, which eventually become part of a dispositif of bodily automatism through practice and learning. Both explicit semantic-discursive instructions and implicit affective-somatic signals and atmospheres play their roles. Moreover, movement permeates the bodies and environments of all participants. Mass movement can be operationalized. The field of transdisciplinary robotics, meanwhile, is attempting to reprogram all of this, which by now seems to be succeeding extraordinarily well. However, rather than marvel at, and succumb to, this triumphant march of a stupid and cheap form of dancing digitality, the important question here is how we ourselves might make the digital danceable for us.

Some of the potential paths are already open: While it is clear that we would need to learn programming instead of just executing commands, to make, maintain, and repair our own networks, infrastructures, systems, devices, and machines, an overall understanding of how commOnistic cooperativity might rhythmize and concretize remains far off. Accordingly, we should accumulate enough prior knowledge for the solidarity-oriented cooperativity to be implemented and also draw conclusions from this knowledge (from cognitive science and neurophysiology) that, in dancing, these generative models in brain and body not only act or react, but rather above all actively predict. Consequently, in order to counter-dance digitality, we would all have to learn how to proactively make predictions and model processes, that is, to practice the future!

The German media scholar Claus Pias (b. 1967) calls those future histories that computer models generate “synthetic history” in reference to the wording by the semi-governmental think tank RAND Corporation. His own more lucid articulation is even better: “utopias are not any longer a thing of fantasy, a historical or prophetic fancy, but rather the structural results of data configurations” (2005, 133). Furthermore, future knowledge, or “knowledge of simulation” as Pias would call it,

> is always furnished with a hypothetical index, and because various people model and simulate the same problem in various ways, what eventually emerges – instead of certainty – is an uncircumventable spectrum of opinions and interpretations. (2011, 52)

Counter-algorhythmic futures, thus, would have to keep the spectrum of information, potentials, opinions, fictions, explanations, and interpretations open and explore them experimentally and artistically. Utopia becomes fugitive. Loosely based on the Austrian-American cyberneticist Heinz von Foerster (1911–2002), information here is neither substance nor commodity (see 1972, 32), but an open, never-ending, adaptive process. More generally, the commodification of information goes hand in hand with a trivialization of the future, which leads to its loss, as Foerster already critically articulated in the 1970s: “with a future not clearly perceived, we do not know how to act with only one certainty left: if we don’t act ourselves, we shall be acted upon” (ibid., 31).

The loss of the future is the ultimate effect of trivialization, which is based first and foremost on the principle of reduction, efficiency increase, and optimization (see ibid., 40; Müggenburg 2021, 130). As Foerster diagnosed, almost everything in US society had already been transformed into trivial machines, that is, into linear deterministic algorithms that could be easily predicted and controlled. Practicing the future, in contrast, would rely on "non-trivial" (Foerster 1972, 40), non-deterministic machines, algorithms, and rule systems which are supposed to operate as "troublemakers" (ibid., 42) in the process. Thus, it is the diversity of the mixture and the troublesome, obstinate, and wayward characteristics inherent in non-trivial models that must be preserved.

Californian counterculture inspired by psychedelics and the cybernetic (see Turner 2006), and the home computer culture based on it, could not escape trivialization by the automatism of capital. This was despite the self-appropriation of the informational means of production, and some already being familiar with the works of Foerster. Nevertheless, pertinent approaches to counter-dancing digitality came from rather different sources, namely from the work of the North American mathematician and computer scientist Seymour Papert (1928–2016). Papert grew up in Johannesburg, South Africa, studied and earned a PhD in mathematics there and then later in Cambridge, England, in the 1950s. He wrote regularly for the journal *Socialist Review* between 1956 and 1958, lived in London, and was an anti-imperialist, socialist, and activist (see 1957). Later, Papert carried out research in Geneva with the developmental psychologist Jean Piaget (1896–1980). In 1963, he moved to the Massachusetts Institute of Technology in Boston, where he collaborated with Marvin Minsky (1927–2016) and developed the Logo programming language.

Logo was aimed primarily at children and teenagers and, according to Papert, was intended to enable playful immersion in the world of mathematics. The core concept was a programmable drawing pen whereby the lines drawn became visible on the screen surface. The pen was often referred to as a "turtle," because Papert modeled the pen after older mobile robotic vehicles, such as those designed by the North American and British cyberneticist William Grey Walter (1910–77). Walter called these machines tortoises (see 1950, 209). Interactive environments such as Logo would provide "micro-worlds" for children (Papert 1980, 125) that would have a similar effect on learning a programming language as that of a trip abroad to study a foreign language (see ibid., 16). Non-discursive varieties of learning should also become operative, and this is where dancing comes in. Papert compares the activity of dancing to the techno-mathematical operativity of the Logo environment, and sees Brazilian samba schools, with their culture of solidarity and flat hierarchies, as models to imitate.

> LOGO environments are like samba schools in some ways ... from the fact that in them mathematics is a real activity that can be shared by novices and experts. The activity is so varied, so discovery-rich, that even in the first day of programming, the student may do something that is new ... to the teacher. (Ibid., 179)

While Papert admits that the Logo environment circa 1980 is not yet mature enough to manifest all this, he also hopes that the "computational samba school" (ibid., 182) will become a reality in the near future. He is thus a strong intellectual ally for the counter-algorhythmic, the algoriddim, and the foolish idea of counter-dancing digitality. Papert's ultimate prefigurative goal was to activate a child's sensorimotor system for learning to program (see ibid., viii). Children would thus learn to dance digitality. Moreover, a computer and the micro-worlds that Logo could generate would help the child externalize, simultaneously observe, and eventually internalize intuitions and assumptions. According to Papert, the reinforcing effects of programmed biases or false assumptions that often arise with modeling could accordingly be made visible, tangible, and measurable, making these negative effects not only accessible to reflection but also iteratively changeable (see ibid., 145). With these approaches at the beginning of the 1980s, Papert founded a discourse and shaped numerous works in computer pedagogy.

Projects like Logo are simultaneously embedded in media-historical transformations as well. The change from structured to object-oriented programming, pertinently described by the

German computer scientist and cultural historian Jörg Pflüger (b. 1948), had a powerful impact here. While up to the end of the 1960s algorithms and software had been written by experts and required an "empathy with the machinic reader" (2004, 283, my translation), i.e., with the hardware, compulsions for optimization and profit increase emerged with the commercialization of software production, which finally led to the industrialization of programming. Thus in the 1960s and 1970s the programmer became devalued, going "from artist to clerk" (ibid., 288, my translation), and the factory-esque, hierarchical organization of work increased (see ibid., 293). This also entailed some terrible conditions which had already been established in the aforementioned late-eighteenth-century factories filled with human computers. Object-oriented programming, which emerged around 1980 at the latest, went along accordingly with attempts to decentralize, to de-hierarchize, and to modularize the programming work again. Along with component-oriented bottom-up processing (see ibid., 297), increasing requirements came up, which became tangible primarily in the emerging field of computer-based digital simulation and modeling. Here Simula emerged, one of the first object-oriented programming languages, which was developed in Norway in the 1960s. On this, Pflüger explains:

> Dealing with simulations requires that one can try out the consequences of decisions made, experiment with alternatives, and successively refine the underlying model. (Ibid., 300, my translation)

This required decomposing, temporalizing, and algorhythmizing, if you like, the tree-like block structure of older programming languages such as ALGOL into networked, operational units that are active or in a waiting state and can interact with each other. In 1981, the US computer magazine *Byte*, which was very popular in its time, devoted an extensive special issue under the title "Smalltalk" to the object-oriented programming language of the same name, developed at the Xerox Palo Alto Research Center in California. Smalltalk is a software to program software and at the same time a formal language with object-based systematics. In its artificial world, objects have names and can receive messages in the form of simple data such as numbers, letters, or binary logic state values, which they process according to an algorithm. Sending messages to objects instantiate them. Objects can furthermore, if programmed to do so, output a message again. The description of an object is called a class, while what happens operationally in the object is called a method. Objects are instances of a single class. A method is what an object does, works on, processes, and produces. When an object receives a message, its method is carried out. With this configuration, a complex, decentralized network of algorithms can be programmed, wherein a meta framework regulates when, how, or under which conditions which class is to be called and later deleted. What the objects do in each case, and what they are capable of, is described in detail in the classes (see Robson 1981). Thus software can firstly be designed, tried out, tested, and varied more easily, which secondly created optimum conditions for agent-based modeling to unfold as a novel way to design computer models.

Finnish media scholar Jussi Parikka's (b. 1976) classic media archaeology of computer viruses and digital contagions (see 2007), as well as his subsequent study of insect media (see 2010), offer greater elaboration on the emergence of distributed intelligence and the obstinate agency of seemingly unimportant insects and utility programs. There is surely some interlinking between the turn to object-oriented programming of the 1980s and the emergence of time-sharing and distributed computing of the 1970s leading to what we now call the Internet. The uncontrollable self-replication of little computational agents, short code snippets meant as utility programs self-routing their way through a computer network, were soon compared with worms and viruses. The transformation of such little agents into malicious creatures "was linked to the increasing importance [of] software and networked computing" and "the need to control" their environments (Parikka 2007, 51). In the late 1970s John F. Shoch (b. 1949) and Jon A. Hupp from Xerox Palo Alto Research Center conducted some well-documented experiments with such strange agents (ibid., 241). These "multimachine worms" as they called them (Shoch and Hupp 1982, 173) showed messages, loaded pictures, or operated as alarm clocks in the affected computers. These were computer programs consisting of several algorithms that distributed themselves over a network of computers, and co-operated together. How they would do this was not always foreseen. These little software agents showed behavior that was unexpected, autonomous, and obstinate.

> Early in our experiments, we encountered a rather puzzling situation. A small worm was left running one night, just exercising the work control mechanism and using a small number of machines. When we returned the next morning, we found dozens of machines dead, apparently crashed. (Ibid., 175)

It is pertinent here that such utility programs were re-labeled, devalued, and "pathologized" (Parikka 2007, 268) as worms and later as viruses, since their utilization was not fully controllable due to the complex behavior that could unfold out of small unrecognized programming mistakes. This sheds light on the authoritarian episteme of control, command, and instrumentation still prevailing in engineering sciences. Of course, little programming mistakes can cause harm and generate huge amounts of damage, as I showed some years ago in another text (Miyazaki 2016), but what drives catastrophic network breakdowns and the spread of viruses is not only due to their behavior, but is also an effect of a much larger and more powerful automatism, namely M-C-M+, which is the dictate to accumulate capital.

At least two further historical scenes of the 1980s would be important for a genealogy of counter-dancing digitality. First, within Hollywood and the just-emerging computer graphics industry, the first simulations of flocks of birds or shoals of fish are created by Craig W. Reynolds (b. 1953) (see Vehlken 2019, 242), inspiring further computational models of complex movement patterns of self-organizing herds, swarms, and clouds. Second, and much more importantly, through the North American computer scientist Philip E. Agre the concept of improvisation and the situated agent found its way into computer science. While Reynolds referred to Papert's Logo and also described core concepts of object-oriented programming, in 1987 his jargon did not seem to know the term agent.

Agre attempted to formalize everyday activities (which he also called routines) from a computational perspective in his PhD thesis "The Dynamic Structure of Everyday Life," defended at the MIT Artificial Intelligence Laboratory in 1988. He distinguished improvisation and situationally adaptive interactive operationalization from fixed (static) algorithms, or (loosely adapted from Foerster) trivial machines: "everyday activity, however routine, is not a matter of mechanically following a plan" (Agre 1988, 57). In order to algorithmically record everyday actions such as the way to the train station, or to program systems that can algorhythmically unfold the necessary operativity, one would not have to recursively analyze, scale, and finally centrally hierarchize, but rather to situate "metabolically," and also in a sensory and interactive way, the operationalization of everyday processes via a continuously updated system which is designed from a decentralized bottom-up perspective (see ibid., 160).

To demonstrate all of this, Agre, in collaboration with David Chapman, programmed a system that they called *Pengi*. This formed a counter-model to *Pengo*, a maze-based arcade game made by the Japanese company Sega in the early 1980s. *Pengo* was reprogrammed by Chapman and formed the environment, the world, in which *Pengi* operated. For Agre, *Pengi* was the prototype, the demonstration, i.e., the prefiguration of an improvising "situated agent" (ibid., 274, 276, 335). In the arcade game

Pengo, the player can use a joystick to move a penguin figure around a two-dimensional playing field with maze corridors. In the process, Pengo is pursued by stinging bees. When stung, the game ends. Both bees and the game character can push away the wall parts of the corridors to use as a projectile to eliminate opponents. The goal of the game character is to eliminate the bees. The player, whom we could also call the operator or worker, must develop strategies to win.

Pengi was not able to detect the visually apparent conditions on the playing field, i.e., the movement of the projectiles and the bees as a whole – that would have been too costly – but rather only the conditions in the necessary peripheral environment. Simple decision-making is based on options selected from a range of pre-programmed movements that could match the peripheral incoming data, before being carried out. This enabled Agre and Chapman to program a system that interacted “improvisationally” with its ever-changing environment. Rather than creating elaborate models of the world and constructing complicated algorithms, *Pengi* relies heavily on its interactions with the world to organize its activities (see Agre 1988, 255). *Pengi* thus forms a prefiguration for a counter-algorhythmic dance, or counter-dance.

Pengi's critical modeling and playful exploration of countermeasures by adopting a decentralized perspective was further characterized by conceptual proximity first to object-oriented programming, second to sensorimotor-cognitive models, and finally, third – through its focus on improvisation – to dance. The potential of the episteme of this object-oriented design of artificial worlds, which was relatively new in the 1980s, was expanded at the latest in the 1990s by Papert students such as Mitchel Resnick (b. 1956). This meant that in the new level of modeling there was now no longer a single agent, but, as was already the case with Reynolds, several agents. However, Resnick reflected these multi-agent models in terms of their pedagogical use. Agent-based models could explain counter-intuitive dynamics, non-linear tipping points, and often even non-trivial machines. Here, improvisation and mass movement became conceptual neighbors and began to dance.

The synergies that emerge in the tension between contact improvisation via algoriddim, and the counter-dances in the spirit of counter-algorhythmic multi-agent improvisation – which I shall go on to describe – should not be neglected, for here we gradually arrive at the core of counter-dancing digitality. Andy Clark, the aforementioned neurophilosopher, articulated these possibilities and opportunities back in the early 2000s, at a time of general enthusiasm for what were then the "new" media technologies of the Internet and computers, using the concept of the "natural-born cyborg."

> Our biological brains, in concert with these new technologies, can thus grow into hybrid minds better able to understand the kinds of systems in which they themselves participate. (2003, 159)

According to Clark, a concrete example of a hybrid network of brain, body, and new technologies that would facilitate understanding of the current technological systems we are connected with is the StarLogo programming language and environment developed by the MIT Media Lab and Resnick in the 1990s (see ibid., 159). Around 30 years later, there are many StarLogo-like projects and the idea of hybrid minds has been embedded into co-constitutive "sensing machines" as Canadian media, sound, and performance artist, producer, and media scholar Chris Salter (b. 1955) argued (2022, 245).

Whereas Logo could be used to program only a single drawing pen (or Turtle), StarLogo's rigorous application of object-oriented programming made it possible to have several thousand agents interact with each other as software objects in an artificial architecture. Contrary to the modeling language Stella (Systems Thinking, Experimental Learning Laboratory with Animation) which emerged from the context of the system dynamics,

StarLogo would not only model the aggregated dynamics, which is operationalized centrally by a mathematical function such as a Lotka-Volterra equation, but would instead make the dynamics of individual entities – for instance in case of a model in the field of population dynamics – decentrally programmable (see Resnick 1994, 93, 35). StarLogo can be used not only to model the foraging behavior of ants, the formation of traffic jams, the spread of forest fires, or even the dynamic configuration of swarms, but it can also be used to pre-program any conceivable dancing object formation and the spatiotemporal dynamics of their interaction at the object level (see ibid., 49–117). It should not be forgotten that models do not solve problems or simplify facts, but can make everything much more extensive and complicated, but also more comprehensible and understandable. Models have their own obstinacy, their own self-will. Precisely because the interaction, the dancing of the agents, became programmable, more insightful conclusions could be drawn about the overall effects of pre-programmed micro-actions.

Treating agents like dancers is not only a strategy that professional choreographers and dancers later pursued, or one that had already resonated with Agre in the late 1980s in terms such as "improvisation." It should not be forgotten that the operationalization of agent-based models by humans was already directly tested by those in Resnick's circle and who were involved in StarLogo!

The idea of experiencing, testing, and rehearsing agent-based models in a bodily and situated way, through role-playing and group exercises in order to better understand them, probably emerged early on during the development of StarLogo. This was also tested at conferences, as later described by Resnick and Uri Wilensky (b. 1955). In a playful gesture, the group exercises were called StarPeople. StarLogo and StarPeople form a hybrid brain-body-media dispositif and ensemble. Here, the primary goal was immersion in complexity through interactive movement games that are also, in the broadest sense, dances. The simplest and often the first exercise for an ad hoc brain-body-media ensemble was the act of decentralized synchronization through hand clapping (see 1998, 157). The next exercise was one of decentralized communication, that is, the decentralized and self-organized formation of groups in networks. To do this, the group was divided into six unevenly distributed subgroups. Each participant had to keep their assigned group – indicated by receiving a piece of paper with a number between one and six – to themselves. The goal of each round of the exercise was to find more group members. In between, their experiences were shared and discussed. The first round started without any restrictions. The groups quickly formed, some loudly announcing their group number. In the second round, a ban on speaking was introduced. Participants began to show each other the pieces of paper, showing cohesion and moving together. In the third round, everyone was blindfolded, and at the same time whispering was allowed. Now it took a long time for the groups to form; often individual participants were "left over" or felt lost. Some developed search strategies by holding hands, for example, forming an elongated structure that allowed them to search the room more quickly. According to Resnick and Wilensky, the three exercise rounds in which different situations of the dispositif – i.e., of communication conditions – were tested and practiced offered reflections on the different role of centralized or decentralized local structures, of chance, probability, of sensorial or physical conditions, and the role of effectiveness or even feasibility of actions in certain constellations (ibid., 161). While the three exercises described here belong to the category of backward modeling because a specific end goal was given, forward modeling is characterized by first defining the rules and algorithms of the agents and then observing what dynamics develop from them. In the exercise for this, the group was divided into two equally-sized subgroups (A and B), each distinguished by visually-obvious elements. Everyone now had to choose a number between one and 10 again and then form into these groups; this time the groups were about the same size. For example, in the case of 60 people participating, there would be six people in a group. Now the exercise begins. Each of the 10 subgroups decides which members they want to exclude. The criterion here is the visually-obvious affiliation (A or B) which had been determined first, before the numbers. The following rules then apply: If more than two thirds of the group belong to the same subgroup, which would be four people in the example, then the remaining third, which would be two people, must leave the group and move into neighboring groups. There the process starts all over again. If the distribution of A or B into a subgroup is even, i.e., three each from A or B, then no one is excluded and the constellation remains (see ibid., 162). The somewhat surprising overall result shows that evenly-distributed subgroups hardly exist and most consist entirely of either A or B within a short time. This effect is due to a "tipping point," as described in the 1970s by Thomas Schelling (1921–2016), North American economist, governmental advisor, and a scientist of governance, if you will (see ibid., 165).

Schelling was still modeling using small tokens, or game pieces, at the time, but the same principles were operative in his model as in those in the StarPeople exercise. Each token was assigned an agency, meaning being assigned a capacity to flip or move. Resnick and Wilensky were particularly interested in the tipping point and how it could be understood from the participants' points of view. It became apparent that it is difficult to make linear extrapolations of the overall effects based only on the logic of individual actions. This is because it is assumed that two-thirds majorities tend to be exceptions and that the distribution remains even. However, the model contradicted these assumptions and showed that even the smallest changes in initial conditions would lead to tipping points. Such tipping points and their effects would then also be responsible for the emergence of segregated neighborhoods (see ibid., 166). While Resnick and Wilensky's enthusiasm for synthesizing agent-based modeling with role-playing blinded them to the misguided use of simulation to legitimize questionable urban policies, it should be emphasized at this point that the StarPeople exercises were specifically not about legitimizing undesirable and unpredictable effects. Instead they were intended to first make these effects discussable, and problems – such as those of the operation of exclusion – experienceable through dance-like role-plays; and second to subsequently emphasize the importance of experimental and playful modeling. Resnick and Wilensky were primarily concerned with the experience that solutions can certainly lie in the operativity of individual agents, but that sometimes seemingly innocuous individual actions can also produce immediately imperceptible effects, and that the connection between action and overall effect often has no direct causality that could be understood by either linear or intuitive means. This knowledge, and the experience gained after practicing these exercises, becomes critical, i.e., decisive, especially when it comes to understanding complex systems, and can be fostered as know-how through dancing brain-body-media ensembles such as those created during the exercises in StarPeople.

If computer models are to be programmed and their operativities as critical modeling and playful exploration are to become part of a counter-dance against the imposition of digitality, then they must never stagnate but always remain mutable. Not an identifying, conservative, and conserving definition of their purpose or use value, but instead what is fundamental is an emphasis on their obstinacy, or more specifically their waywardness and constant variability. Schelling's model of segregation was found to be widely used by government advisors as a justification for their impotence in the face of ethnic or religious segregation in neighborhoods in large cities. However, it can be simultaneously reinterpreted as a call for diversity, that is, for specific urban policies and information campaigns. Schelling's dynamic model of segregation (see 1971, 181) also has its own peculiarities and obstinacy. The following situation applies: The residents of a neighborhood prefer that at least one third of the neighborhood must be populated with people of similar ethnic origin. Notably, this value varies depending on the implementation of the model. Sometimes it is closer to 37%.[3] If the condition were not met, residents would move to another neighborhood. Even this relatively high tolerance for difference causes 50% segregation in the model. The relatively low tipping point, many argued, can hardly be changed. In this sense, the model was long considered proof that population segregation in urban areas could not be prevented. By 2005, however, it became apparent that by changing the conditions under which residents move, an argument could be made for the opposite. Namely, if a second condition is introduced that calls for diversity (see Fossett and Waren 2005, 1912), e.g., in terms of residents, at least a quarter but no more than three quarters of the neighborhood may be identified as similar. Thus, if at least a quarter of the neighborhood is not perceived as different, the resident moves to another neighborhood with higher diversity. Under such conditions, neighborhoods without segregation would be possible within the same framework as in the Schelling model. This hopeful and optimistic turn was popularized in 2014 by the online project Parable of the Polygons. For the aforementioned media scholar Wendy Chun, the model was another reason why, instead of supporting a love for the similar (homophily), a love for the different should be nurtured and strengthened (see 2018, 148). According to her it is therefore necessary to "devise different algorithms" (2021, 3, 239) and to "engage the depth and breadth of learning" (ibid., 245).

3 The playable webpage "The Parable of the Polygons" by Vi Hart and Nicky Case (2014) helped me a lot to understand the Schelling model.

Repertoire

Prefigurational exercises should result in a repertoire of counter-dance that will allow us to understand, comprehend, and experience commOnistic cooperativity. Modeling and computation would not only help to imagine and practice how human needs are to be matched with the "regeneration times" of various goods (see Redecker 2020, 261) (and thereby how these goods would be produced and consumed sustainably, equitably, and in solidarity with others), but also how the dance of expressing, establishing, and satisfying needs could be regulated and performed so that commOnistic cooperativity would not remain a mere thought experiment, but could be implemented and sustained. Here it is again necessary to emphasize the merits of modeling in comparison to other cultural techniques of knowledge production.

The operativity of modeling consists of many known and tried-and-tested media practices and cultural techniques. Modeling is basically an extension of mapping in its simplest sense, namely as a diagrammatic design practice of spatial constellations between subjects, objects, structures, landscapes, inventories, rivers, energies, processes, and networks being made visible, notable, and recordable. Such an extension aims for an operative and temporal, processual, and dynamically interactive mode of representation. Furthermore, mapping is not copying. The goal is not a realistic image of the mapped thing, as would be the case with a high-resolution photograph. Rather, it is about gaining a visual conceptual orientation. "Cognitive mapping" as coined in the late 1980s by Fredric R. Jameson (b. 1934), is about mapping the socio-political environment, the setting, and the situation, i.e., the sociality in which the mapper finds themselves (see 1988b). Readers might recall that Kurz made similar formulations. Jameson noted that the inability to map and learn social processes and structures is as paralyzing to political experience as the analogous inability to map spatially is to experiencing a city (see ibid., 357). To update this thought: skepticism about the idea of modeling social structures and processes with one's own software paralyzes our techno-political agency in the same way that fear of programming makes critical knowledge of algorithmic machinery impossible.

As the German-Jewish philosopher Walter Benjamin (1892–1940) formulated in his theses on the philosophy of history around 1940, the resistance-minded historian must pursue a "constructive principle" where "thinking is crystallized" and the chain of past constellations, processes, and rhythms under investigation halted, creating an "arrest of happening, or … a revolutionary chance in the fight for the oppressed past" (2003, 396, thesis 17). This poetic and constructive activity resists the dominant reality and reveals its history as contingent, as written by the powerful, and wants to oppose it with other archaeologies. Poetry, as Italian philosopher Franco "Bifo" Berardi (b. 1948) put it, inspires the social imagination and political discourse (see 2018, 18). Moten and Harney's social poetics would resonate here strongly. The relationship to technology seems to be a blind spot in Benjamin's theses on the philosophy of history, but it is taken up in his famous essay on the work of art, in which he uses the metaphor of the "dynamite of the split second" (2003, 265) and argues that film, especially the technique of slow motion, sheds light on "entirely new structures of matter" and leads to the discovery of the "optical unconscious" (ibid., 266).

Whereas in classical analog film, optical impressions are broken down into individual frames, recorded on a photochemical medium, and thus their temporal sequence becomes manipulable, in the field of computation and computer modeling, past processes are still relevant, but, as in hand-drawn animation, they do not require a direct connection to real physical processes. Data also gets generated artificially, that is, synthetically. Such data can be fictitious. The model operates regardless. Although film could also produce operations and thus was future-oriented, computer models allow noticeably more properties, settings, factors, sets of rules, and architectures to be tried out, modulated, changed, and varied. This makes the experimental planning, designing, and projecting of futures possible. From a microstructural perspective, simulation models operate in a manner similar to the anthropogenic modes of perception outlined here:[4] New incoming sensory signals are mixed with internally generated forecasts, projections, and predictions, which are then updated accordingly. In a sense, the application of computer models in the context of commOnistic cooperativity would have to operate similarly to learning-adaptive perceptual action in mammals and humans. Similarly, consumption and (pre-)production could get intertwined.

Projective, prefigurative, and imaginative operativity is not only required for the coming years in which we want to learn to dance commOnistic cooperativity, but has been a core element of human communities since time immemorial – as anthropologist David Graeber (1961–2020) pointed out in collaboration with archeologist David Wengrow (b. 1972):

> We all have the capacity to feel bound to people we will probably never meet; to take part in a macro-society which exists most of the time as 'virtual reality', a world of possible relationships with its own rules, roles and structures that are held in the mind and recalled through the cognitive work of image-making and ritual. Foragers may sometimes exist in small groups, but they do not – and probably have not ever – lived in small-scale societies. (2021, 281)

According to Graeber and Wengrow, ever since there have been settlements in which not only hundreds but thousands of people live together, we have been employing a "virtual reality," i.e., the construct of an imagined society that encompasses entire landscapes and continents. While we have always been

4 This rough argument serves to conceive of these two fields together. Certainly, it is actually more the case that computer models provided new perspectives on cognitive science's understanding of human modes of perception.

able to manage this imagining without any advanced technical and technological media, networked computers have been helping us for several decades to think, design, and transact the difficult mental task of better scaling between inter- and trans-personality. Modeling is one of the basic principles here, along with visualization, to test alternative ways of relating, rules (algorithms), roles, institutions, and structures that we want to sustain and "dance."

In April 2022, Italian environmental historian and Marxist Troy Vettese and North American environmental scientist Drew Pendergrass presented the monograph *Half-Earth Socialism: A Plan to Save the Future from Extinction, Climate Change and Pandemics*, which not only offers a clearly articulated critique of current market-driven environmental policies, but is just as much a vehemently negative judgment of the prevailing technosolutionism and the general drive to humanize nature. Instead, first, it demands a "rewilding" and "unbuilding" (2022, 54) of anthropogenic worlds and, second, it attempts to answer the question of the mediation of production and consumption with the procedure of linear programming (see ibid., 100–17), which was developed by the Soviet mathematician Leonid Kantorovich (1912–86). Third, Vettese and Pendergrass were also inspired by Otto Neurath's (1882–1945) ideas on the natural economy and by Stafford Beer's (1926–2002) Cybersyn project (see ibid., 119). They were presumably less concerned with central planning than with the scenario of a socialist-influenced Earth with a multitude of globally-collaborating planners and modelers, all of whom learned the mathematics of linear programming in their basic education. Fourth, they argue for global institutionally-organized vegetarianism, which could massively reduce soil pollution and our environmental impact (see ibid., 80–81). Particularly pertinent to me seems to be their collaboration with game designers Francis Tseng, Son La Pham, and others; they made use of this collaboration to create a more system-dynamic, non-agent-based computer model which was playable in the form of an online interactive card game (Tseng et al. 2022). What would happen if we could play with agent-based models (see e.g., Savic et al. 2020) and in a similar way test out self-organizing commOnistic cooperativity in dance?

Counter-dancing digitality requires solidarity-oriented forms of life that dance a collective self, a "self [that] feminists must code" (Haraway 1991, 163), and an agencement, dispositif, and network of ironic, slightly vulnerable, often deliberately dysfunctional machines that constantly remodel and prefigure the commOnist future. Berlin-based writer and theater director Luise Meier (b. 1985) presumably imagines her "MRX Machine" along similar lines when she writes: "Fuck-Up + Solidarity = Revolution" (2018, 195). Aotearoan dance, media, and music scholar Sally Jane Norman (b. 1953) may have been thinking of Haraway's call for feminists to program new forms of the collective self when she argued for "live coding":

> Live coding is a way of tuning our cognitive and sensory faculties to enfolded layers of micro, meso and macro temporalities, keeping up with or irreverently outwitting machinic and hybrid forms of liveness, gambling with their parameters, valuing agonistic creative engagement with powerful symbolic systems over their docile or numbly passive use. (2016, 126)

Live (living, alive) programming tunes our cognitive-sensory antennae to the polyphonic, multi-layered timing of the algorhythms in our unbearable techno-eco-bio-sphere and moves us away from the passive use of the digitality imposed on us (on "live coding" see also Blackwell et al. 2022). Existing and emerging models and prefigurative systems could result in a collectively programmed, federally organized cosmos of modeling (a massively multiplayer online game for instance) in which we could prepare, design, plan, try out, discard, reflect, discuss, improve, or test the coming transformation, and thereby learn to counter-dance digitality step by step. Allies, comrades, and cooperatives are plentiful, but we would all need to get to know each other better, cooperate, and grow together. Here, too, media history shows that networking processes emerge suddenly. All it takes is a spark.

It is no longer enough to talk about seed forms, "fermentations" (Kurz 1997, 95), and new narratives. The seed forms must become operative, even if for now this often can only happen in virtual reality via computation and modeling. Transference and transduction from the symbolic space would then be the next step, probably running in parallel because the symbolic and the real meet in dancing. However, we must start counter-dancing for this and learn, program, model, rehearse, embody, and constantly adapt new patterns and counter-algorhythms. Everything needs to be in process and progress, rather than in completion. Often there is talk of the power of contagion, but this alone will not be enough for larger transformational processes. The contagious rhythm must not only provide twitches, convulsions, and spasms, but the unidirectional transmission must be intercepted, reinterpreted, criticized, and danced, in a way of active learning. After the revolution it would be crucial to transform and modulate this energy into daily life practice. The enormous potentials and powers that have become achievable through computation and modeling have long since entered performance and theater as a place of lived solidarity (see Menke 2018, 141). Now it is a matter of carefully redirecting and tapping these resources sustainably. Time is running short! Let's learn to dance with, rather than against time!

References

Adamczak, Bini. 2017. *Beziehungsweise Revolution: 1917, 1968 und kommende*. Berlin: Suhrkamp.

Adams, Rick A., Stewart Shipp, and Karl J. Friston. 2013. "Predictions Not Commands: Active Inference in the Motor System." *Brain Structure and Function* 218, no. 3: 611–43.

Agre, Philip E. 1988. *The Dynamic Structure of Everyday Life*. Technical Report 1085. Cambridge, MA: MIT Artificial Intelligence Laboratory.

Andrejevic, Mark. 2007. "Surveillance in the Digital Enclosure." *The Communication Review* 10, no. 4: 295–317.

Angerer, Marie-Luise. 2022. *Nonconscious: On the Affective Synching of Mind and Machine*. Lüneburg: meson press.

Benjamin, Walter. 2003. *Selected Writings, Volume 4: 1938–1940*. Edited by Howard Eiland and Michael W. Jennings. Harvard University Press.

Benkler, Yochai. 2002. "Coase's Penguin, or, Linux and The Nature of the Firm." *The Yale Law Journal* 112, no. 3: 369–446.

Berardi, Franco "Bifo." 2018. *Breathing: Chaos and Poetry*, intervention series 26. Los Angeles: Semiotext(e).

Beverungen, Armin, Philip Mirowski, Edward Nik-Khah, and Jens Schröter. 2019. *Markets*. Lüneburg: meson press.

Blackwell, Alan F., Emma Cocker, Geoff Cox, Alex McLean, and Thor Magnusson. 2022. *Live Coding: A User's Manual*. Cambridge, MA: MIT Press.

Bollier, David, and Silke Helfrich (eds). 2015. *Patterns of Commoning*. Amherst, MA: Levellers Press.

———. 2019. *Free, Fair, and Alive: The Insurgent Power of the Commons*. Gabriola Island, BC: New Society Publishers.

Bratton, Benjamin H. 2016. *The Stack: On Software and Sovereignty*. Cambridge, MA: MIT Press.

Borck, Cornelius. 2018. *Brainwaves: A Cultural History of Electroencephalography*. Translated by Ann Hentschel. London: Routledge.

Brown, Steven. 2022. "Group Dancing as the Evolutionary Origin of Rhythmic Entrainment in Humans." *New Ideas in Psychology* 64: 1–12.

———, Michael J. Martinez, and Lawrence M. Parsons. 2006. "The Neural Basis of Human Dance." *Cerebral Cortex* 16, no. 8: 1157–67.

Butler, Judith. 2002. "What is Critique? An Essay on Foucault's Virtue." In *The Political*, edited by David Ingram, 212–26. Malden, MA: Blackwell.

Christensen, Julia F., Camilo José Cela-Conde, and Antoni Gomila. 2017. "Not All about Sex: Neural and Biobehavioral Functions of Human Dance." *Annals of the New York Academy of Sciences* 1400, no. 1: 8–32.

Chun, Wendy Hui Kyong. 2018. "Queerying Homophily." In *Pattern Discrimination*, edited by Clemens Apprich, Wendy Hui Kyong Chun, Florian Cramer, and Hito Steyerl, 59–97. Lüneburg: meson press.

———. 2021. *Discriminating Data: Correlation, Neighborhoods, and the New Politics of Recognition*. Cambridge, MA: MIT Press.

Clark, Andy. 2003. *Natural-Born Cyborgs: Minds, Technologies, and the Future of Human Intelligence*. Oxford; New York: Oxford University Press.

———. 2016. *Surfing Uncertainty: Prediction, Action, and the Embodied Mind.* Oxford; New York: Oxford University Press.

Daston, Lorraine. 2022. *Rules: A Short History of What We Live By.* Princeton: Princeton University Press.

Daum, Timo, and Sabine Nuss (eds). 2021. *Die unsichtbare Hand des Plans: Koordination und Kalkül im digitalen Kapitalismus*. Berlin: Dietz.

Distelmeyer, Jan. 2022. *Critique of Digitality.* Wiesbaden: Springer. https://doi.org/10.1007/978-3-658-36978-1.

Dyer-Witheford, Nick. 1999. *Cyber-Marx: Cycles and Circuits of Struggle in High-Technology Capitalism*. Urbana: University of Illinois Press.

Federal Ministry of Justice, Germany. 2022. "Basic Law for the Federal Republic of Germany." Translated by C. Tomuschat, D. P. Currie, D. P. Kommers, and R. Kerr, *Gesetze im Internet*. Accessed January 26, 2023. https://www.gesetze-im-internet.de/englisch_gg/englisch_gg.html.

Federici, Silvia. 2004. *Caliban and the Witch: Women, the Body and Primitive Accumulation*. New York: Autonomedia.

Foerster, Heinz von. 1972. "Perception of the Future and the Future of Perception." *Instructional Science* 1, no. 1: 31–43.

Fossett, Mark, and Warren Waren. 2005. "Overlooked Implications of Ethnic Preferences for Residential Segregation in Agent-Based Models." *Urban Studies* 42, no. 11: 1893–1917.

Foucault, Michel. 1984. "What is Enlightenment?" In *The Foucault Reader*, edited by Paul Rabinow, 32–50. New York: Pantheon Books.

Franklin, Seb. 2021. *The Digitally Disposed: Racial Capitalism and the Informatics of Value*. Electronic Mediations 61. Minneapolis: University of Minnesota Press.

Ghraowi, Ayham. 2020. "Dance Rebellion." In Hito Steyerl. *I Will Survive*, edited by Florian Ebner et al., 17–26. Leipzig: Spector Books.

Graeber, David, and David Wengrow. 2021. *The Dawn of Everything: A New History of Humanity.* Dublin: Allen Lane.

Grassmuck, Volker. 2002. *Freie Software: Zwischen Privat- und Gemeineigentum, Themen und Materialien*. Bonn: Bundeszentrale für Politische Bildung.

Haraway, Donna J. 1991. "A Cyborg Manifesto: Science, Technology, and Socialist-Feminism in the Late Twentieth Century (Reprint from 1985)." In *Simians, Cyborgs, and Women: The Reinvention of Nature*, 149–81. New York: Routledge.

———. 2007. *When Species Meet*. Minneapolis: University of Minnesota Press.

Hardin, Garrett. 1968. "The Tragedy of the Commons." *Science* 162, no. 3859: 1243–48.

Harney, Stefano, and Fred Moten. 2013. *The Undercommons: Fugitive Planning & Black Study*. New York: Minor Compositions.

———. 2021. *All Incomplete*. New York: Minor Compositions.

Hart, Vi, and Nicky Case. 2014. "The Parable of the Polygons." *ncase.me*, online game. Accessed January 27, 2022. https://ncase.me/polygons/.

Harvey, David, A. 2018. *Companion to Marx's Capital*, complete edition. London: Verso.

Heinrich, Michael. 2012. *An Introduction to the Three Volumes of Karl Marx's Capital.* New York: Monthly Review Press.

Helfrich, Silke. 2007. "Gemeinschaftsgüter." In *ABC der Alternativen: von "Ästhetik des Widerstands" bis "Ziviler Ungehorsam,"* edited by Ulrich Brand, Bettina Lösch, and Stefan Thimme, 72–73. Hamburg: VSA-Verlag.

Helmholtz, Hermann von. 1850. "Ueber die Methoden, kleinste Zeittheile zu messen, und ihre Anwendung für physiologische Zwecke." *Königsberger naturwissenschaftliche Unterhaltungen* 2/2: 169–189.

Horgan, John. 1994. "Can Science Explain Consciousness?" *Scientific American* 271, no. 1: 88–94.

Jaeggi, Rahel. 2018. *Critique of Forms of Life.* Cambridge, MA: Harvard University Press.

James Steinhoff. 2021. *Automation and Autonomy: Labor, Capital and Machines in the Artificial Intelligence Industry.* Cham: Springer International.

Jameson, Fredric. 1988a. "On Negt and Kluge." *October* 46: 151–77. https://doi.org/10.2307/778684.

———. 1988b. "Cognitive Mapping." In *Marxism and the Interpretation of Culture*, edited by Cary Nelson and Lawrence Grossberg, 347–60. London: Macmillan.

Kittler, Friedrich. 1999. *Gramophone, Film, Typewriter.* Stanford: Stanford University Press.

Klein, Gabriele. 2013. "Dance Theory as a Practice of Critique." In *Dance [and] Theory*, edited by Gabriele Brandstetter and Gabriele Klein, 137–50. Bielefeld: transcript.

Kluge, Alexander, and Oskar Negt. 2014. *History and Obstinacy.* Brooklyn, NY: Zone Books.

Krakauer, John W., Alkis M. Hadjiosif, Jing Xu, Aaron L. Wong, Adrian M. Haith. 2019. "Motor Learning." In *Comprehensive Physiology*, edited by Ronald Terjung, 613–63. Hoboken, NJ: Wiley.

Krämer, Sybille. 2015. *Medium, Messenger, Transmission: An Approach to Media Philosophy.* Translated by Anthony Enns. Amsterdam: Amsterdam University Press.

Kurz, Robert. 1991. *Der Kollaps der Modernisierung: vom Zusammenbruch des Kasernensozialismus zur Krise der Weltökonomie.* Frankfurt am Main: Eichborn.

———. 1997. "Antiökonomie und Antipolitik: Zur Reformulierung der sozialen Emanzipation nach dem Ende des ‚Marxismus'." *Krisis: Beiträge zur kritik der warengesellschaft* 19: 51–105.

Leeker, Martina. 2013. "Automatismen im Tanz: Vom Agenten-Züchten." In *Unsichtbare Hände: Automatismen in Medien-, Technik- und Diskursgeschichte*, edited by Hannelore Bublitz, Irina Kaldrack, Hartmut Winkler, and Theo Röhle, 111–40. Paderborn: Fink.

Lefebvre, Henri. 2004. *Rhythmanalysis: Space, Time and Everyday Life*, London; New York: Continuum.

Leys, Ruth. 2011. "The Turn to Affect: A Critique." *Critical Inquiry* 37, no. 3: 434–72.
Libet, Benjamin. 1985. "Unconscious Cerebral Initiative and the Role of Conscious Will in Voluntary Action." *Behavioral and Brain Sciences* 8, no. 4: 529–39; comments 539–66.
Lima, Cecília de. 2013. "Trans-Meaning – Dance as an Embodied Technology of Perception." *Journal of Dance & Somatic Practices* 5, no. 1: 17–30.
Linebaugh, Peter. 2008. *The Magna Carta Manifesto: Liberties and Commons for All.* Berkeley: University of California Press.
Lovink, Geert. 2003. *My First Recession, Critical Internet Culture in Transition.* Rotterdam: V2_Publishing.
Manning, Erin. 2012. *Always More Than One: Individuation's Dance.* Durham: Duke University Press.
Marx, Karl. 1975 [1844]. "Economic and Philosophical Manuscripts." In *Early Writings*, introduced by Lucio Coletti, translated by Rodney Livingstone and Gregory Benton, 279–400. London: Penguin.
———. 1976 [1867]. *Capital: A Critique of Political Economy*, volume 1. Translated by Ben Fowkes. London; New York: Penguin Books.
Massumi, Brian. 1995. "The Autonomy of Affect." *Cultural Critique*, no. 31: 83–109.
Meier, Luise. 2018. *MRX Maschine*. Berlin: Matthes & Seitz.
Menke, Christoph. 2018. "Kritik und Apologie des Theaters." In *Am Tag der Krise: Kolumnen*, 133–51. Berlin: August Verlag.
Meretz, Stefan. 2001. "Produktivkraftentwicklung und Aufhebung." *Streifzüge*, no. 2/2001: 27–31.
———. 2003. "Zur Theorie des Informationskapitalismus (Teil 1)." *Streifzüge*, no. 1/2003: 31–37.
Miyazaki, Shintaro. 2013. *Algorhythmisiert: eine Medienarchäologie digitaler Signale und (un)erhörter Zeiteffekte*, Berliner (Programm) einer Medienwissenschaft 12. Berlin: Kadmos Kulturverlag.
———. 2016. "Algorhythmic Ecosystems: Neoliberal Couplings and Their Pathogenesis 1960–Present." In *Algorithmic Cultures: Essays on Meaning, Performance and New Technologies*, edited by Robert Seyfert and Jonathan Roberge, 128–39. London: Routledge.
———. 2020. "Counter-Dancing." In *Architecture and Naturing Affairs*, edited by Mihye An and Ludger Hovestadt, 149–57. Basel: Birkhäuser. https://doi.org/10.1515/9783035622164-023
———. 2022. "Counter-Algorhythmics as Prefigurative Dances of Commonism." *Kunstlicht* 43, no. 2, 74–79. https://doi.org/10.18452/25041.
Moten, Fred. 2016. *A Poetics of the Undercommons*. New York: Sputnik & Fizzle.
Müggenburg, Jan. 2021. "From Learning Machines to Learning Humans: How Cybernetic Machine Models Inspired Experimental Pedagogies." *History of Education* 50, no. 1: 112–33.
Negri, Antonio. 1989. *The Politics of Subversion: A Manifesto for the Twenty-First Century.* Cambridge, UK; Cambridge, MA: Polity Press; B. Blackwell.
Nietzsche, Friedrich. 2000. *The Birth of Tragedy.* Oxford: Oxford University Press.

Norman, Sally Jane. 2016. "Setting Live Coding Performance in Wider Historical Contexts." *International Journal of Performance Arts and Digital Media* 12, no. 2: 117–28.

North, Douglass C. 1986. "The New Institutional Economics." *Journal of Institutional and Theoretical Economics (JITE) / Zeitschrift für die gesamte Staatswissenschaft* 142, no. 1: 230–37.

Nuss, Sabine, and Michael Heinrich. 2002. "Freie Software und Kapitalismus." *Streifzüge*, no. 1/2002: 39–43.

Ostrom, Elinor. 1990. *Governing the Commons: The Evolution of Institutions for Collective Action*. New York: Cambridge University Press.

Papert, Seymour. 1957. "40 Years since the Russian Revolution." *Socialist Review* 7, no. 1: 4.

———. 1980. *Mindstorms: Children, Computers, and Powerful Ideas*. New York: Basic Books.

Parikka, Jussi. 2007. *Digital Contagions: A Media Archeology of Computer Viruses*. New York; Bern: Peter Lang.

———. 2010. *Insect Media. An Archaeology of Animals and Technology*. Minneapolis; London: University of Minnesota Press.

Pflüger, Jörg. 2004. "Writing, Building, Growing: Leitvorstellungen der Programmiergeschichte." In *Geschichten der Informatik: Visionen, Paradigmen, Leitmotive*, edited by Hans Dieter Hellige, 275–320. Berlin: Springer.

Phillips, Leigh, and Michal Rozworski. 2019. *The People's Republic of Walmart: How the World's Biggest Corporations Are Laying the Foundation for Socialism*. London: Verso.

Pias, Claus. 2005. "'Thinking about the Unthinkable': The Virtual as a Place of Utopia." In *Thinking Utopia: Steps into Other Worlds*, edited by Jörn Rüsen, Michael Fehr, and Thomas Rieger, 120–35. New York: Berghahn Books.

———. 2011. "On the Epistemology of Computer Simulation." *Zeitschrift Für Medien- und Kulturforschung* 2, no. 1: 29–54.

Polanyi, Karl. 1944. *The Great Transformation*. New York: Farrar & Rinehart.

Pulvermüller, Friedemann, and Luciano Fadiga. 2010. "Active Perception: Sensorimotor Circuits as a Cortical Basis for Language." *Nature Reviews Neuroscience* 11, no. 5: 351–60.

Reckwitz, Andreas. 2002. "Toward a Theory of Social Practices: A Development in Culturalist Theorizing." *European Journal of Social Theory* 5, no. 2: 243–63. https://doi.org/10.1177/13684310222225432.

Redecker, Eva von. 2020. *Revolution für das Leben: Philosophie der neuen Protestformen*. Frankfurt am Main: S. Fischer.

Repp, Bruno H., and Yi-Huang Su. 2013. "Sensorimotor Synchronization: A Review of Recent Research (2006–2012)." *Psychonomic Bulletin & Review* 20, no. 3: 403–52.

Resnick, Mitchel. 1994. *Turtles, Termites, and Traffic Jams: Explorations in Massively Parallel Microworlds*. Cambridge, MA: MIT Press.

———, and Uri Wilensky. 1998. "Diving Into Complexity: Developing Probabilistic Decentralized Thinking Through Role-Playing Activities." *Journal of the Learning Sciences* 7, no. 2: 153–72.

Robson, David. 1981. "Object-Oriented Software Systems." *Byte* 6, no. 8: 74–86.

Rohmann, Gregor. 2013. *Tanzwut: Kosmos, Kirche und Mensch in der Bedeutungsgeschichte eines mittelalterlichen Krankheitskonzepts*. Göttingen: Vandenhoeck & Ruprecht.

Salter, Chris. 2022. *Sensing Machines: How Sensors Shape our Everyday Life*. Cambridge, MA: MIT Press.

Savic, Selena, Viktor Bedö, Michaela Büsse, Yann Martins, and Shintaro Miyazaki. 2020. "Toys for Conviviality. Situating Commoning, Computation and Modelling." *Open Cultural Studies* 4, no. 1: 143–53.

Schelling, Thomas C. 1971. "Dynamic Models of Segregation." *Journal of Mathematical Sociology* 1: 143–86.

Schiesser, Giaco. 2005. "Medien | Kunst | Ausbildung – Über den Eigensinn als künstlerische Produktivkraft." In *SchnittStellen - Basler Beiträge zur Medienwissenschaft*, volume 1, edited by Sigrid Schade, Thomas Sieber, and Georg Christoph Tholen, 257–74. Basel: Schwabe Verlag.

Schmidgen, Henning. 2014a. *Hirn und Zeit. Die Geschichte eines Experiments 1800–1950*. Berlin: Matthes & Seitz.

———. 2014b. *The Helmholtz Curves: Tracing Lost Time*. Translated by Nils F. Schott. New York: Fordham University Press.

Schröter, Jens. 2013. "Das automatische Subjekt: Überlegungen zu einem Begriff von Karl Marx." In *Unsichtbare Hände: Automatismen in Medien-, Technik- und Diskursgeschichte*, edited by Hannelore Bublitz, Irina Kaldrack, and Theo Röhle, 215–56. Paderborn: Fink.

———, and Till A. Heilmann. 2016. "Zum Bonner Programm einer neo-kritischen Medienwissenschaft." *Navigationen – Zeitschrift für Medien- und Kulturwissenschaften* 16, no. 2: 7–36.

Seyfert, Robert. 2011. *Das Leben der Institutionen: Zu einer allgemeinen Theorie der Institutionalisierung*. Weilerswist: Velbrück Wissenschaft.

Shoch, John F., and Jon A Hupp. 1982. "The 'Worm' Programs—Early Experience with a Distributed Computation." *Communications of the ACM* 25, no. 3: 172–80. https://doi.org/10.1145/358453.358455.

Süß, Rahel. 2022. "Horizontal Experimentalism: Rethinking Democratic Resistance." *Philosophy & Social Criticism* 48, no. 8: 1123–39. https://doi.org/10.1177/01914537211033016.

Sutterlütti, Simon, and Stefan Meretz. 2022. *Make Capitalism History: A Practical Framework for Utopia and the Transformation of Society*. Cham: Springer International. https://doi.org/10.1007/978-3-031-14645-9.

Terranova, Tiziana. 2004. *Network Culture: Politics of the Information Age*. London; New York: Pluto Press.

———. 2022. *After the Internet: Digital Networks between Capital and Common*. South Pasadena, CA: Semiotext(e).

Thompson, William. 1824. *An Inquiry into the Principles of the Distribution of Wealth*. London: Longman.

Tseng, Francis, Son La Pham, Spencer Roberts, Lucy Chinen, Prince Shima, Lukas Eigler-Harding, Chiara Di Leone, et al. 2022. *Half Earth Socialism: A Planetary Crisis*

Planning Game, Trust, online game. https://play.half.earth. Accessed 30 January 2023.

Turner, Fred. 2006. *From Counterculture to Cyberculture: Stewart Brand, the Whole Earth Network, and the Rise of Digital Utopianism*. Chicago: University of Chicago Press.

Vehlken, Sebastian. 2019. *Zootechnologies: A Media History of Swarm Research.* Amsterdam: Amsterdam University Press.

Velasco González, Pablo, and Nathaniel Tkacz. 2021. "Blockchain, or, Peer Production Without Guarantees." In *The Handbook of Peer Production*, edited by Mathieu O'Neil, Christian Pentzold, and Sophie Toupin, 238–53. Hoboken, NJ: Wiley.

Vettese, Troy, and Drew Pendergrass. 2022. *Half-Earth Socialism*. London; New York: Verso.

Vogl, Joseph. 2022. *Capital and Ressentiment: A Short Theory of the Present.* Medford: Polity Press.

Walter, W. Grey. 1950. "An Electro-Mechanical 'Animal'." *Dialectica* 4, no. 3: 206–13.

Wark, McKenzie. 2019. *Capital Is Dead: Is This Something Worse?* London: Verso.

———. 2023. *Raving*. Durham, NC: Duke University Press.

www.ingramcontent.com/pod-product-compliance
Ingram Content Group UK Ltd.
Pitfield, Milton Keynes, MK11 3LW, UK
UKHW041952190726
13854UKWH00005B/1916

9 783957 960481